Longman Social Science Studies
EDITOR RICHARD COOTES

SERIES ONE

British Government

an introduction to politics

Philip Gabriel

Longman

Longman
1724-1974

LONGMAN GROUP LIMITED
London
Associated companies, branches and representatives
throughout the world.
© Longman Group Limited 1974

First published 1974

ISBN 0 582 22134 X

Filmset by Photoprint Plates Limited, Rayleigh, Essex.
Printed in Hong Kong by Dai Nippon Printing Co. (H.K.) Ltd.

Acknowledgements
We are grateful to the following for permission to reproduce copyright material:
House of Lords for extracts from *Hansard*, vol. 153, January 1948, and vol. 280,
February 1967; Parliamentary Profile Services Limited for an extract from
Business Background of MPs, by A. Roth, 1963; Macmillan, London and
Basingstoke for an NOP table from *The British General Election of 1970* by
David Butler; The Observer for extracts from an interview with Harold Wilson
by Kenneth Harris of *The Observer Magazine*, 24th October 1965. London
Express News and Feature Services for extracts from *The Daily Express* and
The Evening Standard dated 18th June 1970; Associated Newspapers Group
Ltd for an extract from *The Daily Mail* dated 18th June 1970; The Observer
for an extract from *The Observer* dated 18th June 1970.
  For permission to reproduce photographs we are grateful to:
Associated Press, page 91; Associated Television Corporation Ltd, page 78;
Peter Baker, pages 95 and 104 *right;* Klaus Barisch, page 76; Barnaby's Picture
Library, page 104 *left;* British Broadcasting Corporation, page 72; Camera
Press, pages 4, 7, 23 *top left,* 28, 53 *middle* and 59 both; Central Office of Infor-
mation, Crown (c), page 34; Central Press Photos, pages 41 *centre* and 53 *top*;
Civil and Public Service's Association, page 43; Conservative Central Office,
page 23 *centre*; Fox Photos Ltd, page 50 *bottom*; Her Majesty's Stationery
Office, Crown (c), pages 42 *bottom* and 58; Keystone Press Agency Ltd, pages 1,
10, 14 *right,* 18, 26, 31, 41 *top,* 44, 47, 49, 53 *bottom*, 62, 66, 67, 71, 74, 75, 79
and 80; Labour Party Photograph Library, pages 13, 21, 23 *top and centre right
and bottom left*, 54, 57 and 84; London Express Pictures, page 35; National
Portrait Gallery, page 11; Press Association Ltd, pages 3, 23 *bottom right*, 27
bottom, 36, 48, 56 and 68; Punch, page 8; Radio Times Hulton Picture Library,
pages 6, 16, 19, 83, 86, 100 and 101; Richmond Golf Club, page 5 *right*; Sirlin
Studio, Sacramento, page 15; The Times, page 85; Topix, page 92; United Press
International, pages 41 *bottom* and 96; United States Information Service, page
5 *left*; Western Mail and Echo Ltd, Cardiff, page 14 *left*.

Contents

Preface

SOCIAL SCIENCE STUDIES is a three-part series which aims to provide attractive introductory material in sociology, politics and economics for CSE courses and for those students working at a similar level in further education General Studies. The authors of the series believe that these perspectives (along with social anthropology) should provide much of the core of social education, and that they have been too long neglected at this level.

The four books of *Series 1* are designed to introduce readers to basic concepts and approaches in each field, together with methods of enquiry and sources of information available to the social scientist. The shorter books of *Series 2* cover specific topics, some of which develop out of themes opened up in the basic texts. Finally, *Series 3* consists of short, illustrated booklets, dealing with contemporary social, political and economic issues *as they arise*. The ten to twelve titles produced each year supplement the texts in Series 1 and 2 with up-to-date information, analysis and discussion; and give something of 'the news behind the news'.

Despite its wide scope, this series is not offered as an all-inclusive course. Most schools and colleges have resources of 'raw data' available, including statistics, press cuttings, articles and gobbets from more advanced books, and it is assumed that teachers will continue to use these. But by its nature such material has not usually been written with young people in mind. Consequently there are often difficulties over language and a seeming lack of structure in many of the topics studied.

The present series aims to give needed *shape* and *direction* to the study of society at this level. And at every stage great care has been taken to keep the language clear and straightforward. The series also aims to provide a springboard for further reading and research, and to this end it is hoped that the 'To write, discuss and find out' sections will prove useful.

Richard Cootes

BRITISH GOVERNMENT aims to go beyond the rather formal, descriptive approach which is often found in books at this level. Although the main institutions of central government are examined in detail, they are seen as part of a dynamic political system. This means that such elements as power, conflict, compromise and decision-making are woven into the structure of the book and illustrated, whenever possible, with practical examples. Politics can be a fascinating, even exciting, study and it is hoped that this book will go some way towards encouraging the reader to find it so.

Thanks are due to Richard Cootes, an enthusiastic and painstaking editor, and Jacqueline Mair, for their valuable suggestions. The author alone is responsible for any remaining imperfections.

Philip Gabriel

What is politics?

Imagine that a group of young people want to go out for the afternoon, but that there is some disagreement as to whether they should go to a football match or the cinema. How would they reach a decision? If they are willing to split up there is of course no problem. But what would happen if they wanted to stay together yet could not agree?

Perhaps they would take a vote, with the decision depending on the majority. But would everyone have an equal vote? There might be an accepted 'leader', who usually has a bigger say than the other members of the group.

Possibly some of the group do not mind where they go, and are willing to leave the decision to those who feel more strongly about it. In the end, perhaps it is suggested that they should all go to a café instead; and, to avoid further argument, everyone agrees. Alternatively they might argue all afternoon and go nowhere.

Politics is closely concerned with decision making among groups. Here we see a typical way of reaching a decision: by a show of hands at a mass meeting.

Groups, decisions and politics

We are all familiar with situations like this because we all belong to groups of various kinds. And from time to time *decisions* have to be made. Some groups we belong to are fairly small, such as a family, a school or college class, or a youth club. Other groups, including trade unions, towns or whole nations, are very large, and each member can only get to know a few others personally. But, large or small, all groups are faced with problems of decision-making.

Different groups manage their affairs in different ways. To take an extreme case, television gangsters (and presumably those in the real world too) usually have a 'boss' who imposes his will by force. He allows no questioning of orders, and certainly would not let the gang decide anything for him. This is one way of arriving at decisions. Another way is to take a vote, after discussion and argument, and accept the point of view of the majority. There are many other alternatives which are a mixture of the two, and in the end our group of friends might settle for one of these.

Now our example does in fact illustrate some of the basic problems of politics. Politics is partly concerned with *how groups reach decisions, and carry them out*. In other words, it is concerned not only with the decisions themselves but with the *ways* in which they are arrived at. However when we speak of 'politics' we do not usually think of decision-making among small, informal groups like the friends in our example. What sorts of groups *do* we have in mind? To help answer this question, let us consider two imaginary examples of the different kinds of groups to which people belong:

Mr Smith works for a *bus company*, and is a member of the *Transport and General Workers' Union*. He has a *family*—a wife and two children. He is secretary of his local *angling club*, and often goes for a drink with his *friends at the local pub*. He is a member of the *Labour Party* and thinks of himself as belonging to the *working class*.

Mr Jones owns a small *engineering firm*. His *family* consists of a wife and three children. He is vice-president of the local *golf club*, and has *friends round for bridge* twice a week. He goes to *church* regularly, belongs to the *Conservative Party* and considers himself a member of the *middle class*.

Some of these groups—including the golf and angling clubs, the church and the trade union—are highly organised. They have formal rules about the selection of officials, the rights and duties of members, and so forth. On the other hand, groups such as families, friends in the pub or at the bridge table, and the 'working' and 'middle' classes, are *in*formal. They still have rules, standards or shared ways of doing things, but these are not laid down in any precise way.

Is it the formal, organised kind of group that we have in mind when we speak of 'politics'? After all, people talk of the 'politics of the boardroom' (the place where company directors meet) or even the 'politics of the golf club'. In such cases 'politics' usually means discussion and argument about decisions or about people who are (or aim to be) in positions of leadership. For instance it might be Jones's ambition to become president of the golf club, and a number of members may be trying to whip up support for him because they are dissatisfied with the existing president.

It is certainly possible to think of politics in this way. But as a rule we think of political decisions as those which affect *the general arrangements of society*. Of all the groups that Smith and Jones belong to, only the Labour and Conservative Parties are mainly interested in decision-making for society as a whole. Their aim is to govern; to carry out their policies for organising the day-to-day life of the nation (or, in the case of local government, the population of a particular region). Many other kinds of groups, including Smith's trade union and Jones's firm, will want to *influence* the government. But they do not seek to control

A political meeting. This one was part of a by-election campaign in Macclesfield, September 1971.

and shape the life of the nation in the way that political parties do.

It is politics in this familiar sense—the ways in which the affairs of society are managed—that we shall be concentrating on in this book. However we shall not be looking just at the activities of political parties and politicians. All sorts of other groups and individuals take part in political activity and help to shape the society we live in.

Should we count heads or break them?

If we go back to Smith and Jones for a moment, we can see that there are sharp conflicts of interest between some of the groups they belong to. One is a trade unionist, the other is an employer; one is Labour, the other Conservative. Furthermore, either Smith or Jones may face conflicts of their own. Smith's family might object to the time he spends with his friends in the pub. Or it could happen that Jones's engineering firm is criticised by his Conservative friends on the local council for polluting a river or disposing of scrap metal untidily.

Because there are so many groups in society,

each wanting different things, government is a difficult business — both at national and local level. It is much more complicated, for example, than a group of friends trying to decide where to go on a Saturday afternoon. If the friends fail to agree they can easily split up, some going to the cinema and some to the football match. But in the wider society it would be disastrous if groups that disagreed went their separate ways. For instance it is vital that managers and workers in industry should co-operate with each other, in spite of their disputes.

So groups and individuals who disagree must find ways of living and working together if society is not to break down. This is a basic problem of politics; and, to put it very simply, there are two sorts of solutions. One way of dealing with people who disagree with us is to shoot them, hit them over the head or lock them up. This approach can be used by conflicting groups within a society, or by a government which gives out orders and uses force to eliminate opposition.

The other kind of solution to the problem of conflict is the one generally favoured in most societies. It is to work out methods of decision-making which all groups can accept as fair—

3

even when they do not get their own way. At government level, this is only likely to work if the groups directly concerned in particular decisions are *consulted*. Every man likes to feel that he can at least express his point of view. And without proper consultation there is always a danger that decisions will not be accepted.

When groups are in conflict in our society they normally rule out violence as a way of settling their differences. It is accepted that each individual has a right to his own views. But the recent history of Northern Ireland provides a bitter and bloody exception—as this picture shows. Here opposing groups have resorted to force, because of disagreements about who should have political power and how the country should be governed.

RULES

THE RICHMOND GOLF CLUB is established to promote the interests of the Game of Golf, and shall consist of not more than four hundred Full Members, exclusive of Five-day and other Members.

Management of the Club

1. (*a*)   The Management of the Club shall be in the hands of a Committee consisting (subject as hereinafter provided) of the Captain, 9 Ordinary Members and 3 Additional Members.

   (*b*)   The Captain shall be nominated by the Committee of the Club and shall be elected at the Annual General Meeting. Any two Full Members of the Club shall be at liberty to put forward a Full Member to serve as Captain having previously received his assent.   The name of each member so put forward shall be sent in writing to the Secretary six weeks at least before the Annual General Meeting.   The Committee in making their nomination shall have due regard to the names of all members so put forward.

   (*c*)   Every Ordinary Member of the Committee (not being a member elected to fill a casual vacancy) shall be elected for a term expiring on the day of the third Annual General Meeting held after the Annual General Meeting at which he was elected as such member, and shall not be eligible for re-election until the Annual General Meeting following the Annual General Meeting at which he last ceased to be such a member.

   (*d*)   The Additional Members shall be as follows:—

     i   One member shall be appointed for a period of three years by the Five day Members of the Club, the mode of appointment to be from time to time prescribed by the Committee;

     ii   One member shall be appointed for a period of three years by the Lessees of the lease granted by the Crown;

   3

Two contrasting examples of written constitutions: above, *part of the laws controlling the government of the USA;* right, *the rules of a golf club.*

A political system which allows disagreements to be openly expressed can only work if all conflicting groups have one important thing in common—*toleration* of each other. Everyone has to accept that others have a right to be different and to hold opposing views. So long as there is this basic toleration, a society can be governed peacefully despite clashes of interest between various groups within it.

Laws and conventions

We have seen that all groups have rules or standards, but that it is usually only in formal or 'organised' groups that some rules are written down. For example it may be a written rule that Smith's angling club elects its president every year. In the same way, most governments have to keep to written rules, or *laws*, which set limits on what they do. Such rules collected together (perhaps in a single document) are known as a CONSTITUTION*

Nevertheless, even where rules are written down, certain customs, habits or 'unwritten rules' usually develop alongside them. For instance even though it is in the constitution of Smith's club that the president is elected annually, it might be the custom to return the existing president unopposed, if he is willing to stand. In politics we call this kind of custom or habit a CONVENTION.

The British political system is based on a mixture of laws and conventions. Many of the conventions are vitally important, and essential to an understanding of the way government works. For instance according to the *law* the Queen still has just as much power as her predecessors in centuries past. But in practice it is a *convention* of British politics that the

---

*The meanings of words printed in CAPITALS in the text are summarised in the Glossary of Basic Terms.

Laws often protect people from exploitation. For instance Factory Acts put a stop to the sorts of working conditions shown here—in the Sheffield steel industry of the 1860s.

prime minister and his Cabinet should rule on her behalf—as 'Her Majesty's Government'.

Although over the years Parliament has passed very few laws controlling its own activities, it is of course continually making laws to control *our* lives. In a sense, every law restricts the freedom of the individual. But this is not as sinister as it sounds. If people were free to do anything they liked, there would be no peace and security and the weak would be at the mercy of the strong. Laws which take away the 'freedom' to murder, steal or swindle are in fact designed to *increase* the freedom of the vast majority, by deterring such behaviour.

Laws of this kind are 'negative', in the sense that they prevent people from doing certain things that are thought undesirable. Other

sorts of laws are more 'positive', such as those giving free education to the young or financial help to old people, the sick and the unemployed. These services cost money, of course, which means that taxes have to be imposed. Does taxation limit our freedom, by preventing us from spending our money as we would like? In one sense the answer is yes. But without taxes there could be no 'positive' laws freeing people from poverty, from sickness, and so forth.

Obviously laws only have an effect if most people obey them. But why are laws obeyed? Is it simply because people are afraid of the consequences of breaking them? This is always an important reason, but there is more to it than that. After all, if everyone decided to break a certain law it could not be enforced, and would soon cease to exist. To a large extent laws are obeyed because most people accept that they are for the benefit of society. This in turn means that laws must be seen to be necessary and fair. In any civilised country there will only be respect for the law if it reflects the basic attitudes and values of the people. So in the end the real strength behind the law is public opinion.

Majorities and minorities

We have seen that conflict between groups need not disrupt a society so long as there is basic agreement about how decisions should be made. In Britain and many other countries it is generally accepted that the majority should decide. And in order to find out what the majority view is, elections are held from time to time, and groups and individuals are consulted in various other ways.

Why do we attach so much importance to the wishes of the majority? After all, on some issues there might be 'experts' who know far more than the average person. They could easily take decisions on their own, without having to bother about getting a majority on their side. At first sight this might seem a good idea. But in practice there is usually a good deal of dispute about who the 'experts' are. And experts can usually be found to support either side of an argument. Besides, most political issues involve *moral* judgments about what people ought and

ought not to do, and what is good for society. In such matters of conscience there can be no 'experts'.

Where decisions are not based on the wishes of the majority, some people will have more say than others. It could be that they are wiser, but it is more likely to be because they are richer and stronger. Minority governments often assume that they know what is best for the majority without bothering to ask them, through elections and so forth. Or they deliberately use their power to advance their own interests. This happens in some countries where a white minority rules a majority of black people and allows them little or no say in political affairs.

In one sense even the British people are ruled by a minority, because in modern society only a few people can be directly involved in government. We choose representatives (Mem-

Black South Africans being hustled by police outside a courtroom in Johannesburg (1956). South Africa is ruled by a white minority, and this kind of government generally has to use force in order to control the majority.

bers of Parliament and local councillors) to act on our behalf. But at least these representatives are *appointed* by the majority—and *dismissed* by them. This means that any politician who wants to gain power, or retain it, must take account of the views of ordinary people. In the end, if majority decisions turn out badly at least the responsibility for them will be widely shared. People are more likely to accept the failures as well as the successes of governments chosen by a majority vote.

Political power

Political activity is of course not just concerned with making decisions but also with carrying them out. Those who are responsible for managing the affairs of a society require some sort of *power* in order to make their decisions effective. Consequently the study of politics is to a large extent a study of the power that some men have over others—the forms it takes, the groups or individuals who possess it, and the uses to which it is put.

Those who seek political power are often talked of in uncomplimentary ways. Politicians are accused of being 'power mad', and we are told that power corrupts people, making them dishonest and self-seeking. It is always easy to claim that politicians want power in order to 'feather their own nests' or simply to feel important. But we cannot get away from the fact that in a modern state *some people* have to take essential decisions; and they have to be given power to carry them out.

Everyone has views about what is good or bad in society, and about the sorts of changes that need to be made. Political power is essential if any such changes are to be brought about. The really important question is not whether some men should have power over others, but whether power is put to good use. Are political leaders taking account of the wishes of the people? And if they are not is it possible to replace them by peaceful means?

Political power is not always to be found in

THE LEVER BREAKS

Groups outside the 'formal' system of government often have a great deal of political power. This Punch *cartoon was drawn at the time of the General Strike, 1926, when nearly 4 million men downed tools and brought the industrial life of Britain to a standstill. It represents the view of the Government, that the unions were trying to overthrow the parliamentary system—a charge that the unions strongly denied.*

the most obvious places. In Britain for example it might seem that political power is largely concentrated in the hands of MPs at Westminster. But in fact many groups and individuals outside Parliament have power to influence political decisions, including leaders of big business, the trade unions and the civil service. So when we look at the British political system we should keep firmly in mind the question 'Where does power lie?'

To write, discuss and find out

1a Make a list of the groups you belong to, and then distinguish between 'formal' and 'informal' ones.

b Taking each group in turn, describe its method or methods of making decisions.

2 Some of the groups that Smith and Jones belong to are regularly in conflict. But what basic belief do they all share? Why is this so important for our society?

3 Choose an example of a 'formal' group that you belong to, and illustrate the difference between written rules and conventions.

4a In what sense do laws *increase* people's freedom?

b Imagine there were no laws controlling the behaviour of car drivers. Describe in as much detail as you can the difficulties that would result.

5 In what circumstances do you think the violent overthrow of a government would be most likely to occur? Can such violent revolution ever be right?

6a Which of the following acts would you consider to be 'wrong'? List them in order of 'seriousness'.

Not keeping a secret told to you by a friend
A homeless family 'squatting' in an empty house
Sex before marriage
Killing an enemy soldier
Telling lies to your parents
Betraying your country to an enemy because you believe its leaders are evil and corrupt (as some Germans did in World War Two)
Not voting in an election
Breaking a speed limit on a public highway
Stealing apples from an orchard
Not paying your fare on a bus
Which of these acts are *illegal*, and which are not?

b Can you explain why there are no laws against some things that are generally thought to be wrong?

7 Are there any political issues which you think should be decided by 'experts' rather than politicians or the people in general? What are the main objections to this kind of government?

8 'Guy Fawkes was the only man who ever entered Parliament with good intentions.' Do you agree that we should distrust people who seek political power? If so, why?

We all know that there are many different ways of organising a political system. Some countries are monarchies, others are republics; some have presidents, others have prime ministers. Most countries have ways of electing representatives to some kind of assembly or parliament, although the methods of election and the powers given to representatives vary a great deal. The number of political parties varies too. There may be several major parties, as in Italy; two main ones, as in Britain and the USA, or only one party, as in Communist states and many African countries.

All these organised ways of doing things are what we call INSTITUTIONS (systems of rules, standards and customs that are known and expected within a particular society). Each country has its own distinctive political institutions, which form the basic framework of government. In Britain these include the monarchy, the two Houses of Parliament, the method of electing MPs and the Cabinet, headed by a prime minister.

The Duke of Kent opens the parliament of the former British colony of Uganda (1962). Several newly independent African states tried to copy European forms of government, with little success. A country's political system needs to be rooted in its own history and traditions.

However institutions of this kind are often only 'surface features' of a political system. To understand a nation's form of government properly we need to dig more deeply and examine the *underlying beliefs and principles* which back it up. These in turn will depend on the history and traditions of the people.

In the case of Britain, many political institutions date back to the Middle Ages. But this does not mean of course that we are governed in the same way as the people of medieval times. The political power of the Crown and the House of Lords has been transferred to members of the Commons, and the British people have more influence on decision-making than ever before. These and other changes reflect important shifts in political attitudes.

Some basic questions

The true character of a system of government can best be discovered if we look beyond the outward forms of its constitution and examine the answers to certain basic questions such as the following:

a Are there ways of changing rulers and policies without the need for violence and bloodshed?

b Are there laws to protect the weak from exploitation by the strong?

c Are there real opportunities for ordinary people to express their political opinions openly, and are they encouraged to do this? And, perhaps most important of all,

d Is real power in the hands of a minority, or are the people as a whole able to exercise political influence?

These questions draw attention to the underlying principles behind *any* form of government. But as far as Britain is concerned we shall see that the answers to all four questions have changed completely over the past 300 years or so. If we take the first three—peaceful change of rulers, laws to protect minorities, and freedom of opinions—the foundations for these were

James II, King of England, 1685–88. He was driven from the throne when his own subjects invited the Dutch King and Queen, William and Mary, to come and 'restore the liberties of Englishmen'. After 1688, the United Kingdom never again needed a revolution to change its government.

laid in the seventeenth and eighteenth centuries. The fourth—growth of the political power of ordinary people—is a development of the nineteenth and twentieth centuries.

We now pride ourselves on the peaceful and orderly way in which we change our government. And we are quick to defend freedom of speech and the protection of the rights of individuals, whether they be rich or poor, weak or strong. But in the seventeenth century and before it was not like this. Within the space of fifty years, beginning in the 1640s, a struggle for power between Parliament and the Monarchy led to civil war, the execution of Charles I, the setting up of a republic under Oliver Cromwell, and the banishing of another King, James II. In these years Britain was the most revolutionary state in Europe! Breaking heads was a more usual way of deciding major disputes than counting them, and many people were afraid to express their opinions for fear of being persecuted.

After the deposing of James II in 1688, the United Kingdom never again needed a revolution to change its government. The political troubles of the seventeenth century gave rise to a freer, more peaceful society, in which people for the most part learned to tolerate each other's political views.

Nevertheless in the eighteenth century political power was still firmly in the hands of a privileged few. Only about 250,000 of the nation's most influential citizens had the right to vote, and both Houses of Parliament were dominated by the landowning nobility and gentry. Since then, of course, the wealthy and privileged have given way to the demands of the mass of the people for a share of political power. To understand how this came about we need to take account of far reaching changes in our society in the last 200 years.

Government in an industrial society

Of all the factors which have helped to shape the present British political system, the most important is the growth of large-scale industry and town living. In the mid-eighteenth century the great majority of people lived in remote villages or small market towns, farming the land or working in village trades. Cloth-making and the manufacture of metal goods—the chief industries apart from agriculture—were carried on in cottages and small workshops. Husband, wife and children worked together at home.

Such home or 'domestic' industries began to decline about 200 years ago. The reason was the introduction of large water-powered, and later steam-driven, machines, first of all in cloth-making. To make effective use of powered machinery it was necessary for workers to be collected together in factories. By the end of the eighteenth century the age of mass production had begun. And as large-scale industry developed, Britain's population became increasingly concentrated in towns and cities—mainly in the coalfield areas of the Midlands and the North of England, South Wales and Central Scotland. These changes led to the transformation of the political system, along with every other aspect of national life.

The growth of large-scale industry and commerce helped to create two new and powerful groups in Britain: first, a middle class made wealthy by the ownership of factories, mines, banks, shipping and so forth, and, second, a town based working class. The old political system, with power in the hands of the landowning nobility, was gradually transformed under pressure from these two groups.

In the nineteenth century the right to vote was extended to the new middle class (and later to ordinary workmen) and many Parliamentary seats were redistributed from country areas to growing industrial towns. Political leaders increasingly came from the middle class, rather than the old landed gentry. These 'new men' in politics mostly joined the Liberal Party. But in the early twentieth century, as the power of the Liberals declined, the industrial and commercial middle class became a major force in the Conservative Party.

Meanwhile, the spread of factory industry meant that large numbers of working men were brought together in one place. They toiled long hours for low wages, just as they had done before the Machine Age. But now that they worked and lived together in large groups, they began to realise the power they could possess if they *acted together* to improve their pay and working conditions. If all the workmen in a factory asked for the same thing, and refused to go on with their jobs unless they got it, they would be in a strong bargaining position with their employers. So trade unions were formed, and members used their most powerful weapon —a threatened stoppage of work, or *strike*—to

gain improvements in their standard of living.

This large industrial working class, increasingly organised into trade unions, became a strong political influence by the end of the nineteenth century. In 1900 some unions and other groups formed a Labour Representation Committee, to work for the election of MPs who would represent working people in Parliament. After the 1906 election, when it won twenty-nine seats, it was renamed the Labour Party. The two major parties were still the Liberals and Conservatives. But within twenty years Labour replaced the Liberals as the main opposition to the Conservatives.

As Britain became a complicated industrial society, governments took on many new responsibilities. A hundred years or so ago it was believed that governments should concentrate on a limited range of activities, and the spending of money by the state should be kept as low as possible. So the government merely kept peace and order, and looked after British interests at

The Labour Party arose at the turn of the century, to represent the industrial working classes in Parliament. In 1924 it formed the government for the first time—under Ramsay MacDonald, whose Cabinet is pictured here.

home and abroad. For the rest the people attended to their own affairs. There was no question of the state providing social services and schemes of welfare for those in need. People had to sink or swim on their own.

Nowadays of course the role of government is quite different. We live in what is often called a 'Welfare State', in which vast amounts of money are collected in taxes and used to pay for all kinds of social services, including medical treatment, social security and education. And things like fuel, power and transport services, on which the whole community depends, are no longer run for private profit but by public bodies under the general supervision of government ministers.

13

In Wales and Scotland there are Nationalist Parties demanding independence. Gwynfor Evans (left) sat in Parliament as a Welsh Nationalist, 1966–70, and Winifred Ewing (above) was a Scottish Nationalist MP, 1967–70. She was returned again in 1974 along with six other Scottish Nationalists and two Welsh Nationalists.

Hand in hand with industrial development in modern society goes the development of towns and cities—what we call *urban* areas. Greater London alone accounts for nearly a fifth of the population of the United Kingdom. Consequently many political issues arise out of the problems and needs of an urban society—housing, slum clearance, traffic congestion, pollution and so on. Furthermore, because industry has not developed evenly across the country, but has become heavily concentrated in certain areas, there is a regional pattern to British politics. This is illustrated here:

Main areas of Labour support, 1970 election		
	Total number of seats contested	Seats returning Labour MPs
North of England	326	212
Scotland	71	44
Wales	36	27

The bulk of Labour voters belong to the industrial working classes. So the 'safest'

Labour seats are in industrial areas, especially those which developed in the nineteenth century —Northern England, South Wales and Central Scotland. These are also the areas where there are problems of declining industries and unemployment. The Conservatives can usually count on winning most seats in rural areas, and they are very strong in smaller towns and in the suburbs of larger cities.

As well as differences between regions of the United Kingdom, there is still a great gulf between the living standards of the very rich and the very poor. Modern social services have eliminated most of the worst poverty, yet millions of families still find it hard to make ends meet. Britain. is still a class conscious society. We have seen that most of those who think of themselves as working class vote Labour. Similarly, the majority of people calling themselves middle or upper class vote Conservative (see Chapter 12).

A unified society

Despite its divisions, Britain (excluding North-

As in all states of the USA, the Californian Assembly (shown here) makes its own laws in many important areas of government.

ern Ireland) is in many ways a highly unified society. People are not deeply divided by language, race or religion—at least not to the extent that different groups in the community find it impossible to exist side by side. The basic unity of the British people is assisted by well developed communications. Roads, railways, postal and telephone services link all corners of the nation more quickly and cheaply than in most other industrial societies.

A large part of the *mass media* (TV, radio, the press and so on) covers the whole of mainland Britain. Often the same TV programmes are shown from Cornwall to Aberdeen. (This is not so in a large country like the USA, where scores of different companies broadcast to local regions and there are few 'coast to coast' programmes.) Although politics may not be followed with the same enthusiasm as racing, football, quiz or comedy programmes, the major issues are given great prominence in the

mass media. Indeed, political comment and discussion is a basic concern of the mass media, and to this extent they are part of the political system in modern society.

In larger, less unified countries, such as the USA, Australia or India, separate regions or states have important political powers which the central government cannot touch. These are called 'federal' states. In the USA, for example, the individual states—California, New York, Texas and so on—can make their own laws governing many areas of life, including education, marriage and divorce, and the treatment of criminals.

In the United Kingdom, on the other hand, political power is concentrated in the hands of

Coronation of Queen Elizabeth II in Westminster Abbey, June 1953. Many parts of the ceremony go back to the Middle Ages, thus illustrating a vitally important feature of the British political system: continuity with the past.

the *central* government, through its control of Parliament. It is true that there are elected councils in each locality, which help to administer education, certain health and welfare services, minor roads and so forth.* But these powers were given by Parliament in the first place. The British Parliament is supreme, and if it wishes it can change or abolish the whole system of local government. No political institutions in our society are beyond the reach of Parliament.

Continuity with the past

A time-traveller returning to Britain after 500 years absence might be very surprised to find that, on the surface at least, many of our political institutions have hardly changed. We still have a monarch, crowned at Westminster in much the same way as William the Conqueror and his successors were after 1066. We still have the two Houses of Parliament. In the Lords, the Chancellor sits on a Woolsack—reminder of the great medieval woollen cloth industry—and in the Commons, MPs grant taxes just as knights of the shires and citizens of the towns did in the thirteenth century. Even our local government system of councils and mayors has its roots in the Middle Ages.

*See *Local Government* (Series 2)

But if our visitor were to look beyond these outward forms of the constitution, and ask himself the sorts of questions raised at the start of this chapter, he would realise that our system of government had been transformed in his absence. *Real political power* has shifted from the Crown and the House of Lords to MPs elected by all the people.

These changes have for the most part come about peacefully, apart from the violent struggle between Crown and Parliament in the seventeenth century. In other countries many bloody revolutions have been needed to produce a similar transfer of power. One of the reasons for the slow evolution (gradual change) of the British political system is the fact that in modern times Britain has neither been invaded nor defeated in a major war. Our good fortune is largely due to the existence of the sea as a natural frontier. The last foreign invasion was that of William the Conqueror in 1066. The French and the Germans, on the other hand, have suffered both invasion and conquest *twice* since 1870. On each occasion they have been led to rethink completely the way they govern themselves.

Nearly all countries have had to make 'fresh starts' after conquest or revolutions. And for this reason most have a written constitution which sets out the workings of government in minute detail. The USA and USSR made 'fresh starts' after revolution in 1776 and 1917 respectively. Germany's present system of government dates from the postwar period of the late 1940s, as does that of China. And France has had two completely different constitutions since the last war.

Because for centuries past Britain has not experienced a 'clean break' in its political history, no new constitution has been written from scratch. There is no single document or set of documents which could be called 'The British Constitution'. Instead there is a series of Acts of Parliament, legal decisions and conventions which have accumulated over the centuries. They all illustrate a most important feature of the British political system — continuity with the past.

To write, discuss and find out

1   Outline some of the ways in which the growth of large-scale industry and commerce has affected British politics in the last 200 years.

2   What are the main factors which (a) divide and (b) unite the British people?

3   Can you explain why the British political system is so strongly rooted in the past (compared with that of most other nations)?

4   *Find out* about the important constitutional changes that followed the English Revolution of 1688.

5   *Find out* about the decline of the Liberal Party in Britain in the years following World War One.

Much of this chapter deals with the historical background to the British political system. However only the briefest of surveys can be attempted in a book of this kind. To follow up the main topics touched on here you should turn to more detailed accounts in history books (one or two are recommended in the Further Study section on p. 106, and you may already know others).

Voting and elections

Many organised groups hold elections, which give their members a chance to support or reject the people previously chosen for office. School club or national government, the idea is the same. At some stage those who are given power must answer for their actions. Indeed, voting at elections is the most obvious way in which people take part in political activity. However it is important for them to feel that elections are not the *only* way of influencing leaders or officials. Between elections, those who hold office usually try to keep in touch with the views of the 'rank and file', and, if possible, consult them before major policies are decided. If this does not happen, and a gulf appears between what people want and what elected officers do, then the same officers are unlikely to be chosen next time.

Representation

But why *do* we elect officers of a club, or Members of Parliament to represent us? The same principle holds good for most organised groups. We need people to make decisions *on our behalf*, because it would be impossible for everyone to be directly involved every time a decision is called for.

It might be possible in a small village to gather everyone together occasionally when a major decision has to be taken. But this method could

Nearby residents protesting at the opening of a new motorway in London, 1970. There is little that they personally can do about it. They hope to get their political representatives to act on their behalf.

The right to vote

A suffragette is arrested during a demonstration outside Buckingham Palace, 1914.

Today almost everyone over eighteen in the United Kingdom is entitled to vote in elections. The few exceptions to this include Peers (members of the House of Lords) and inmates of prisons and mental homes. This explains why the graph below does not quite reach 100 per cent.

But it is only in recent times that voting rights have come to be distributed equally among the adult population. At the beginning of the nineteenth century, the right to vote was a privilege enjoyed by less than $\frac{1}{2}$ million of the nation's most influential male citizens.

A series of 'Reform Acts' between 1832 and 1884 extended voting rights to a majority of males, but still no woman could vote.

Women could vote for County and County Borough Councils after 1888, and they were allowed to become councillors in 1907, but they played no part in central government. To remedy this, the Women's Social and Political Union (WSPU) was founded in 1903, with the aim of organising public demonstrations in favour of women's *suffrage* (voting rights). Members were soon known as 'suffragettes'. They began heckling speakers at political meetings, organising petitions and even chaining themselves to railings outside the houses of Cabinet ministers.

During World War One (1914–1918) large numbers of women were employed in essential industries, including armaments factories. This valuable work achieved more than the campaign of the WSPU, and immediately after the war women's suffrage was granted. Even then the voting age for women was kept at thirty – they did not reach equality with men, voting at twenty-one, until 1928.

Up to 1948, some people were entitled to vote twice. There were 'university seats' where graduates could vote in addition to their own constituencies. The abolition of this 'plural voting' meant that the election of 1950 was the first to be fought on the basis of 'one man, one vote'.

Parliamentary reform acts

Percentage of population over 20 entitled to vote

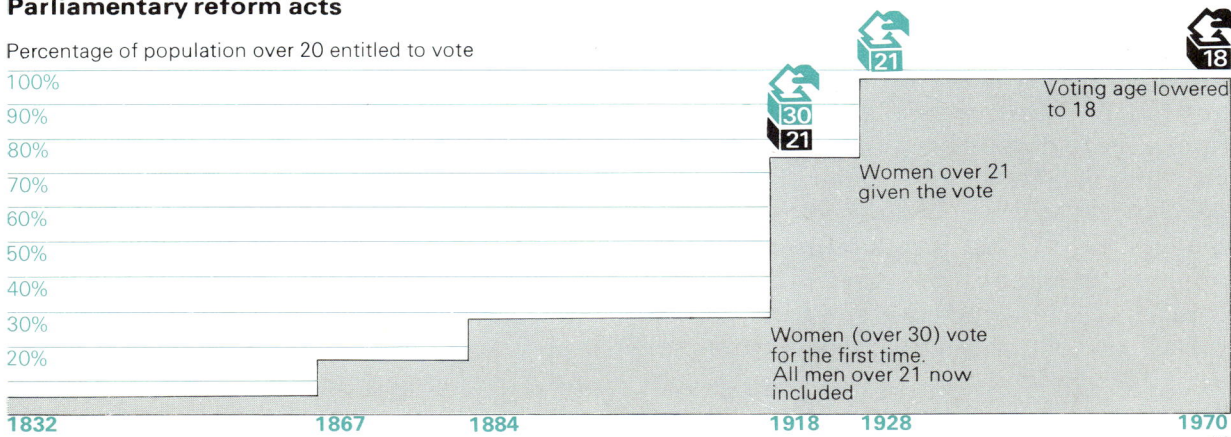

Voting age lowered to 18

Women over 21 given the vote

Women (over 30) vote for the first time. All men over 21 now included

| 1832 | 1867 | 1884 | 1918 | 1928 | 1970 |

not be applied to larger communities. The wide variety of complicated decisions which face national or local government could not be decided every time by this kind of direct consultation. It would be expensive, time consuming and difficult to reduce issues to a simple 'yes' or 'no'.

For the purpose of representation in national government we elect MPs (Members of Parliament) who usually belong to a political party. Although representation is important, it does not mean that MPs are elected just to express the views of the people and never to think for themselves. To begin with, how do we define 'the view of the people' at any given moment, on any given issue? It is often extremely difficult to find out the majority view, and, in any case, should the MP be concerned with the majority view in the country, his party, or his local constituency? Often they will not be the same.

We expect an MP to take account of the wishes of the various groups he represents, but also to act according to his own conscience. At some stage he will have to present himself to his electorate and explain his actions and those of his party. We generally want MPs who are responsible individuals, willing to use their own judgment—even though we usually vote for them because of their 'party label'.

The British electoral system

Constituencies

For general elections, when we choose both MPs and a government, the country is divided into roughly equal areas called 'constituencies'. Ideally, each constituency should have about the same number of voters. But this is often difficult to achieve, because of population changes and the fact that rural constituencies would become too large in area if they had to equal the electorate in cities and towns. So the size of electorates can vary considerably. In the 1974 election, the scattered rural constituency of the Western Isles, in Scotland, had

an electorate of only 22,307, whereas the urban constituency of Daventry in Northants had 83,000 electors.

It is an important feature of the British electoral system that the successful candidate is. simply the one with the most votes, even though a majority of the electors may not have supported him. In seats where there are three or more candidates, the winner will often get a lot less than 50 per cent of the votes. Here is an example from the 1974 election:

		percentage vote
Colne Valley (Yorks)	Labour	39.9
	Liberal	38.1
	Conservative	22.0

Something else follows from this. A national political party may attract millions of voters yet win very few seats, if its support is thinly spread. This point is illustrated by the performance of the Liberal Party in the 1974 election:

	Votes cast	*No. of MPs*
Conservative	11,928,677	296
Labour	11,661,488	301
Liberal	6,056,713	14
	Average vote per MP	
Conservative	40,299	
Labour	38,742	
Liberal	432,622	

Even though the Liberals have a large following in the nation as a whole, their chances of becoming a major party in Parliament are remote. This is because there are few constituencies where the Liberal vote is strongly concentrated. Our electoral system gives an advantage to the larger parties, and penalises smaller ones. However it does usually give the governing party an effective majority of MPs in the House of Commons. Only once since 1945 has a government had to rely on the support of a second party—despite the fact that in this period no ruling party has won 50 per cent of the total votes cast. The British electoral system puts the stress on strong one-party government, rather than on producing the closest possible relationship between votes cast and seats won.

How are party candidates selected?

In all parliamentary seats, members of each political party form a *local constituency party* (Conservatives prefer the term 'association'). These bodies have the power to select candidates. If a party does not at present hold the seat, or if its present MP is not standing again, a 'short list' of four or five names is chosen by the officials of the constituency party. This has to be approved by local members, and by national officials of the party, after which a selection conference is held. The listed candidates make a short speech, and answer questions from an audience of party members. Then a vote is taken. There is no need for a candidate to be born in, or to live in, the constituency. Many people, ambitious to become MPs, will apply all over the country for consideration.

This system of selecting candidates gives considerable power to the local constituency parties. About 75 per cent of all seats can be regarded as 'safe'. In other words, one particular party is virtually certain of winning each time there is an election. In such cases, the constituency party meeting, which may only consist of a few dozen people, is not only selecting a candidate, but also picking the MP. A 'safe' Labour seat for example may have over 25,000 Labour voters, but only active members of the party will play a part in deciding the candidate. Few 'safe' Labour seats have an active party membership of more than 1000, and most have less than 500. The actual selection meeting consists of delegates chosen by these active members.

It is very rare for a sitting MP not to be chosen to stand again—assuming he wants to. Constituency parties usually re-adopt the MP without any opposition. So when an election occurs, the majority of MPs know that they will be both re-adopted and re-elected. However

S. O. Davies, late MP for Merthyr Tydfil, who retained his seat in 1970 at the age of 84.

sometimes there can be an upset. In the 1970 election the Merthyr Tydfil Labour Party refused to re-adopt the sitting MP, Mr S. O. Davies, because they felt he was too old. Mr Davies had the final say. He fought the election as 'Independent Labour', and won by over 7000 votes.

Election preparations

Marginal seats

If over 450 seats are 'safe' for one main party, it is clear that any election campaign will be concentrated on those seats most likely to be won or lost. These are the 'marginal' seats, which will decide the election. In 1970 the Conservatives, by a net gain of sixty-six seats, changed a Labour majority of ninety-seven in 1966 into a Conservative majority of thirty-one. This was a big victory, yet the key to the whole campaign lay in less than 100 constituencies.

In the two years before the election, the Conservatives deliberately concentrated their attention on the Labour held marginals, and their policy was fully justified by the results.

The timing of an election

This is the prime minister's decision, although by the 1911 Parliament Act, he *must* call an election within five years of the last one. He will try to judge the time in order to give his party the best possible advantage. Most prime ministers will try to 'go to the country' when the economy is doing well, people have money in their pockets, and the unemployment level is low. And because the government has a great deal of influence on the state of the economy, this gives the ruling party a distinct advantage.

In recent years, the increase in the number of opinion polls has also affected election timing. For instance the sudden recovery of support for the Labour Government early in 1970, as shown in the opinion polls, encouraged the Prime Minister to have an election in June of that year. In fact it was not essential for him to call an election before March 1971.

The national campaign 'build-up'

The most important part of the election campaign, apart from special efforts in marginal seats, is at national level. Most people vote according to party labels, rather than the personality and ability of individual candidates. They link themselves to a political party, to some of its national policies and some of its national leaders. The vast majority of voters never attend any kind of constituency meeting, nor indeed know very much about their local candidates.

National campaigns usually start well before the election date is known. All parties think carefully about the policies they intend to put before the voters. Party committees investigate different areas—social services, industrial relations, foreign affairs and so forth—in order to produce a range of policies typical of that particular party. Clearly there must be detailed discussions both inside the party and with interested groups outside it. For instance the Labour Party would want to know trade union attitudes towards industrial relations.

As election time approaches, party propaganda becomes more hectic, with considerable sums of money being spent on advertising, through newspapers, posters, leaflets and car-stickers. Party 'allies' will do the same. In 1963–64 the Conservative campaign cost over £1 million, but an extra £2 million was spent in support of certain Conservative policies by groups such as Aims of Industry and the Economic League. In the summer of 1969 the Labour Party spent £200,000 on advertising; and £120,000 in the four weeks before the election was announced in 1970. Although Labour is supported financially by the trade unions, it usually has less money to spend.

Until the actual announcement of the election and the dissolution of Parliament—on average 28–35 days before polling day—there are no legal limits to how much a party and its allies may spend on campaigning. Parties are not allowed to buy advertising time on television, but they do use other media, especially the press and outdoor poster hoardings. Once the election is announced there are strict regulations governing party spending in constituencies. They must not spend more than £750 plus 5*p* for each six electors in rural seats, and £750 plus 5*p* for each eight electors in urban seats. Proper accounts have to be produced. Considering the vast sums spent before the campaign, this might appear a strange limitation. It was imposed to stop money being spent on bribing electors—an old English custom!

Pre-election work in constituencies

Most party work at this level is concerned with local affairs—council problems, fund raising, membership and social activities, with council elections as a major activity between general elections. Although national issues and national leaders are the most important factors in deciding the result of a general election, the

more marginal the seat, the more important other factors become. In the end victory may go to the party with the best local organisation for getting its supporters to turn out and vote.

Every February a new Register of Electors is published for each area. This contains the name, address and electoral number of those entitled to vote in local and general elections. The first task of a well organised constituency party is to find out the voting intentions of everyone on that list. This is done through 'canvassing'—going round every door and asking people how they intend voting. Canvassing is a method of finding out people's intentions, not of persuading them. The chances of converting someone in a brief doorstep chat are remote.

The results of the canvass are marked on cards, as 'For', 'Against' or 'Don't know'. In addition, people who need a postal vote are discovered. This means that if they are ill, have moved from another constituency or are likely to be away, a ballot paper is sent to them. In a marginal seat the party with the most efficient method of finding its postal vote supporters may win for this reason alone. Canvassing also determines how many people will need transport to the polls; and it finds those willing to display posters, or join the party and help in a more positive way. It is rare to have a fully canvassed Register, although this is obviously the ideal to work towards. Canvassing continues almost up to election day itself.

Meanwhile the candidate will get to know the area, discover its problems, and meet as many people as possible. He will try to get publicity in the local press and, above all, whip up enthusiasm amongst party workers. In other words, he will carefully 'nurse' the seat. Existing MPs have an obvious advantage here, because of appearances on radio and television, and because their speeches in the Commons will probably be reported in the local press.

The campaign

Once the prime minister announces the date of the election, all parties go into a frenzy of activity. The main aim is maximum publicity for their leaders and policies. Each party's *manifesto* is published, setting out its main policies. Even though most people are unlikely to read the manifesto or even a shortened version, the party that wins the election will claim that it has a *mandate*—a right to pursue the policies it put forward.

Party political broadcasts

Time is set aside by the BBC and ITV for the parties to use as they think best. The content and form of the programmes is decided and paid for by the parties, and time is allocated according to party strength in the country.

In addition to official election broadcasts, there will be extensive cover of the campaign in news and current affairs programmes, 'election specials' and the like. In fact the party leaders, rather than the party manifestos, tend to receive the greatest publicity. In news broadcasts during the 1970 election campaign, information about Mr Wilson took up 56 per cent of time given to the Labour party, and information about Mr Heath 60 per cent of the time given to the Conservatives.

The press

Unlike television, which tries to be neutral, the press is almost totally committed to one side or the other. Nevertheless, most politicians agree that *any* publicity, even if unfavourable, is better than none at all. Each party usually holds a press conference every morning, to drive home its main policies and to answer charges from the other side. Under cross-examination from journalists—not all of it friendly—party spokesmen have another opportunity to get into radio and television news, and the evening papers.

Opinion polls appear more frequently at election time, and are greeted with the same anxiety as a sick man's temperature. During the 1974 campaign, ten polls were published regularly. Such polls may influence the prime minister's timing, but there is no evidence to

Political Broadcasts, 1970

Time per broadcast
5 minutes
10 minutes

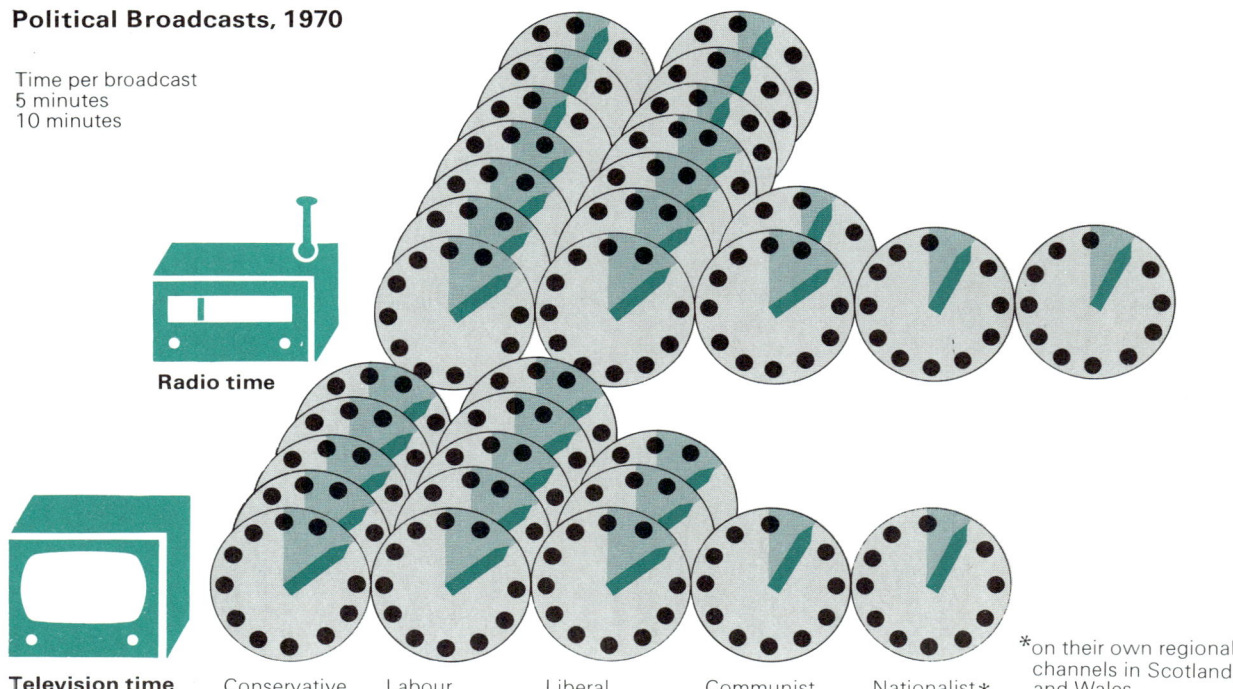

Radio time

Television time

Conservative   Labour   Liberal   Communist   Nationalist *

*on their own regional channels in Scotland and Wales

suggest that they affect the way people vote. Both in 1970 and in 1974 the polls forecast a comfortable win for the government of the day. They were wrong both times. In 1970 it appears there was a last minute switch of voters to the Conservatives, and this was not recorded because the interviews had taken place a few days earlier. In 1974 the polls were right in forecasting more Conservative voters than Labour but the majority was less than expected and not translated into a majority of seats. If polls have any value, it is in measuring the effectiveness of a campaign. In 1970 the Conservatives made little progress at first, and their poor showing in the polls was a factor which led them to conduct a last minute attack on rising prices.

The campaign in the constituencies

The constituency parties all engage in similar activities in the weeks leading up to polling day. Candidates are required to hand in nomination papers, and to pay £150 as a deposit, which they lose if they get less than one-eighth of the total vote. This is done to discourage frivolous candidates. Each candidate sends his election address to the voters, in which he introduces himself and outlines party policies. He will work ceaselessly to meet people at doorsteps, factory gates, street corners and so on. Public meetings are held, and are usually badly attended unless a well-known national speaker is present. But at least the speeches are well reported in the press. For party workers it is a time of great excitement, even if most people are unmoved and anxious for life and television to return to normal.

The key time in a constituency is obviously election day itself, when the organisation of the party, or lack of it, really matters. Ideally by this time canvassing will be over, with the 'Don't knows' revisited; and all known party supporters will have been listed. These are now concentrated on. The diagram overleaf illustrates the usual method of 'getting out the vote' in each part of a constituency.

Results

Polling stations close at 10 p.m. The ballot boxes are sealed and sent to a central place,

Reporters put questions and hear policy statements at a Conservative press conference during the 1970 election campaign.

ELECTION 70

Evening Standard

London: Thursday June 18 1970

Ted comes up on the rails

This is the final poll forecast of the Opinion Research Centre

THE GENERAL ELECTION of 1970 looks like a photo-finish.

The injection of disturbing trade figures in the last few days as a major issue has turned the campaign into a pollster's nightmare.

Scotland may well be swinging away against the Tory Party and the West Midlands perhaps swinging towards them.

The one thing which opinion polls do not like is a close finish. For normal sampling error means that they may not be many percentage points away from the result—but still pick the wrong winner.

However, these are the figures

VOTING INTENTION

	1966 General Election 4th June	1970 11th June	Now
Lab.	48.1	47	45½
Con.	41.4	43	46½
Lib.	8.6	6	6
Other	1.9	4	2
Lab. lead	6.7	4	—
Con. lead	—	—	1

Never in the past has the electorate been so volatile or the opinion polls performed such somersaults. Within five weeks the swing has gone from a half...

Daily Mail

THURSDAY, JUNE 18, 1970

PRICE 6d.

NOP NATIONAL OPINION POLLS

Labour's lead down to 4 p.c.

WITH only five days of the campaign left, the Gallup poll in today's *Sunday Telegraph* shows the Conservative trailing Labour by only 2.5 per cent. According to Gallup, Labour's lead has been cut by three-quarters in a week.

It remains to be seen whether Gallup is only a mirage or whether the Tories have at last sighted water in the desert. All the other polls completed this week show Labour lead of 12.4 per cent. The Labour lead of 12.4 per cent, by contrast by NOP would give Labour a Commons lead over the Tories of 1945 dimensions—about 180.

THE OBSERVER

Established 1791
No. 9,335 Price 1s 3d

14 JUNE 1970

Today's poll verdict: 100-seat majority for Wilson

by ANTHONY KING

THE OBSERVER'S POLL ANALYSIS

Poll	N.O.P. (Daily Mail) %	Harris (Daily Express) %	O.R.C. (Evening Standard) %	Gallup (Sunday Telegraph) %	Weighted Average %	1966 (excl. N. Ireland) %
LAB.	51.6	49	49	48.0	49.5	48.8
CONS.	39.2	42	42	45.5	42.2	41.5
LIB.	7.9	8	8	5.5	7.3	16.1
Other	1.3	1	1	1.0	1.0	6.4
(Don't know)	(9.4)	(9)	(9)	9.1		
Lab. lead	12.4	7	7	2.5	7.3	7.3
Interviews began	12 days ago	11 days ago	10 days ago	7 days ago		**7.3** % Lab. lead
No. interviewed	2,373	2,617	965	2,336		

Monday, is 7.3 per cent (see table). This is the same lead Labour enjoyed in 1966. It would give Mr Wilson an overall Commons majority of 100 compared with the present 65.

The Gallup-NOP discrepancy is one of the largest ever recorded. The timing of the interviews cannot explain it entirely. More probably, it signals a genuine movement towards the Tories is exaggerated in Gallup by normal sampling fluctuation. Similarly, NOP was almost certainly exaggerating Labour's lead—even when the interviews were taken a week ago.

Gallup's findings, running counter to the trend, are the most recent. Interviewing began last Sunday, three days after the interviewing for the Opinion Research Centre poll in the Evening Standard, which reported Labour still 7 points ahead.

The average Labour lead, based on all four polls completed since

Gallup cannot be checked against the ORC's usual 'stop-press' poll in the Sunday Times. The poll was cancelled because of the newspaper strike.

Before today's Gallup findings appeared, Conservative spokesmen seemed desperately anxious to clutch at straws. Mr Anthony Barber, the party chairman, pointed at yesterday's Tory press conference that experienced psephologists reported a sharp swing to the Conservatives in the marginals despite the opinion polls.

He also cited a number of polls in the provinces. A *Sunday* survey in the West Midlands, published in the *Birmingham Post*, did show the Conservatives regaining Oldbury and Halesowen, but it also indicated that Labour would comfortably hold two key marginals in Birmingham.

Mr Barber's claim that the Tories would capture three Bradford North turned out to be based, not on a sample survey at all but on a straw poll conducted by a Yorkshire Post reporter.

There is still no hard evidence that Labour will suffer from a low turnout. NOP reports that more certain than Labour supporters are 'very likely' to vote. But the gap is small—83 per cent to 84—and would, at most, cut Labour's lead by only two points.

Moreover, as Mr Wilson foresaw, the pattern of holiday-making should work to Labour's advantage. British Travel Association surveys show that the two-thirds of people in Britain who take holidays away from home are heavily middle- and upper-middle class. Nearly 20 per cent of all holiday-makers start their holidays in June.

DAILY EXPRESS

THURSDAY JUNE 18 1970

No. 21,778
Weather: Sunny spells, showers
Price 6d.

Final Harris Poll shows it's getting closer

By WILFRID SENDALL

A LABOUR lead of two per cent nationally, but with clear evidence that the Tories are ahead in the marginals—this is the last word in today's Daily Express Harris poll.

It signals a desperately close finish to today's General Election and predicts deadlock in the new House of Commons.

The final Harris Poll forecast of votes:

	%
Labour	49
Conservative	47
Liberal	...
Nat. & other	...

Labour lead ...

On the basis of a two per cent lead nationally, an analysis of 39 to 25 in the swing

NOW PICK THE WINNER!

THIS IS THE DAY

Method of 'getting out the vote'

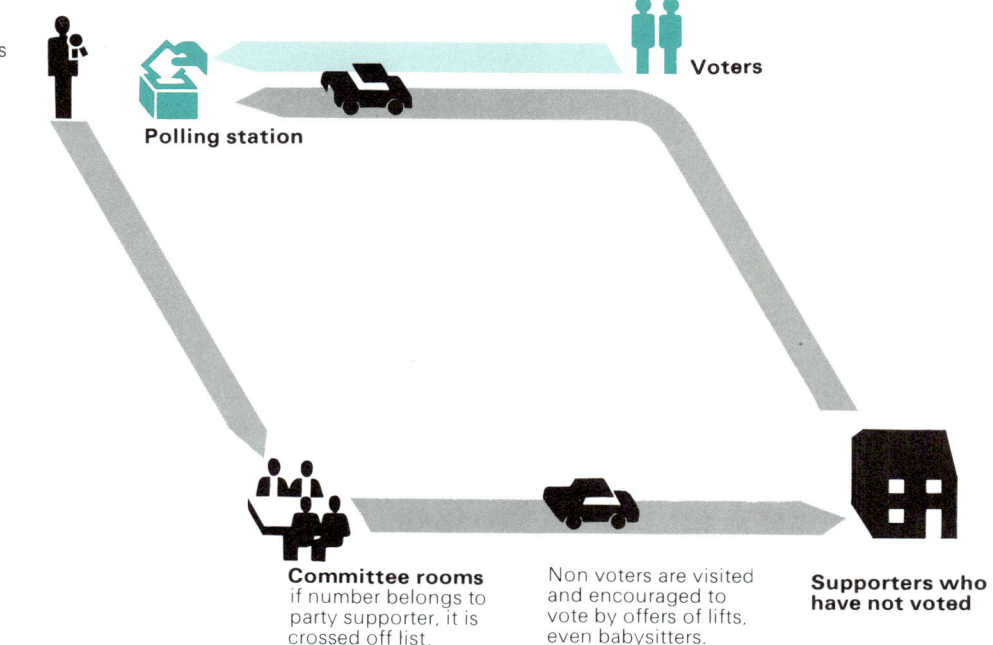

Party recorder
makes a note of voter's electoral number and sends it to committee rooms

Polling station

Voters

Committee rooms
if number belongs to party supporter, it is crossed off list.

Non voters are visited and encouraged to vote by offers of lifts, even babysitters.

Supporters who have not voted

Above *Obviously this system of getting party supporters to the polling station depends on* finding them *in the first place, during door to door canvassing.*
Below *An election result being announced by the returning officer.*

often a Town Hall, for the count. The first results may be known in just over an hour, although some rural constituencies do not start counting until the next morning. If a result is close—either in deciding the winner or in saving a deposit—there will be a recount. In Peter-borough the 1966 election produced eight recounts and a final majority of three for Sir Harmer Nicholls (Conservative).

If one party wins a decisive victory, the result of the election will be known within a few hours. If the government has been defeated, the prime minister will resign and the leader of the new majority party will be invited by the Queen to form a government.

The importance of elections

However unsatisfactory certain aspects of our electoral system may be, it does ensure that governments can be removed peacefully; that political change can occur without the use of violence. The voters are able to choose between different political parties, and the parties accept the decision. In many other countries no such choice is offered, so frustration against a government cannot be expressed in elections. In such cases violence may appear to be the only remedy.

Having won an election, a government can reasonably claim that it has the right to exercise power over the people. In this sense an election provides a government with legal and moral *authority* for carrying out its policies. Although many voters show little interest in elections, at least the politicians take them seriously. They carefully examine their policies and make great efforts to explain them to the electorate. Parties and politicians are forced to take a serious look at *themselves*, as their own weaknesses are exposed by their opponents.

Elections provide us with our representatives. They give each individual a particular person to represent him in Parliament. Although we tend to associate MPs with parties, they do spend a considerable amount of their time looking after the problems and complaints of individuals. Elections are the one time when the vast majority of people take part in political activity. Roughly three-quarters of the people vote; and in the process they are encouraged to think about the kind of government they want.

Not all governments are removed peacefully, through the ballot box. In 1973 the elected leaders of Chile were overthrown in a military uprising. Here we see soldiers in the streets of Santiago, the capital city.

The House of Commons, 1945–74

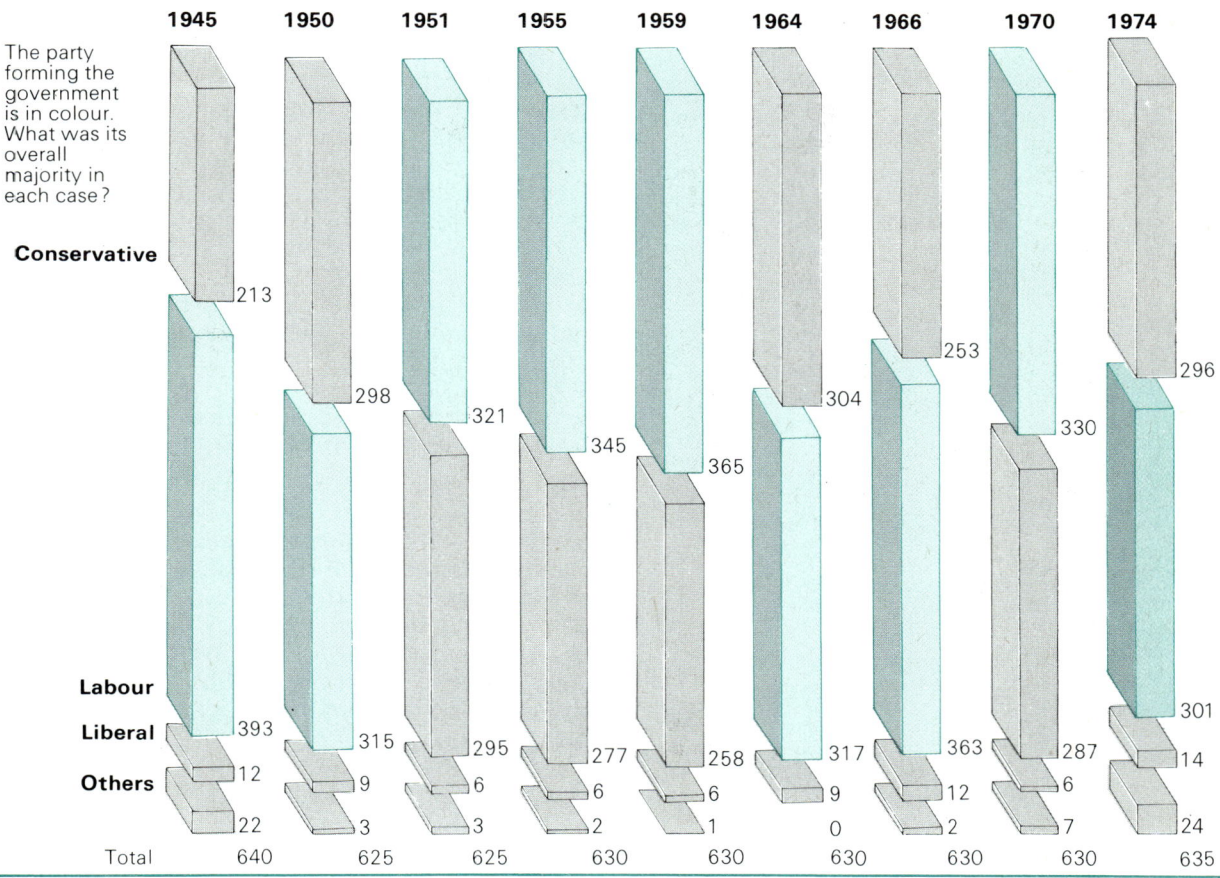

The party forming the government is in colour. What was its overall majority in each case?

	1945	1950	1951	1955	1959	1964	1966	1970	1974
Conservative	213	298	321	345	365	304	253	330	296
Labour	393	315	295	277	258	317	363	287	301
Liberal	12	9	6	6	6	9	12	6	14
Others	22	3	3	2	1	0	2	7	24
Total	640	625	625	630	630	630	630	630	635

Election results, 1945–74

	Electorate and turnout	Votes cast	Conser-vative	Labour	Liberal	National-ist†	Commu-nist	Others	Swing to Con (%)
1945	73·3% 32 836 419	100% 24 082 612	39·8% 9 577 667	48·3% 11 632 891	9·1% 2 197 191	0·6% 138 415	0·4% 102 760	1·8% 433 688	
1950	84·0% 34 269 770	100% 28 772 671	43·5% 12 502 567	46·1% 13 266 592	9·1% 2 621 548	0·6% 173 161	0·3% 91 746	0·4% 117 057	+2·9
1951	82·5% 34 645 573	100% 28 595 668	48·0% 13 717 538	48·8% 13 948 605	2·5% 730 556	0·5% 145 521	0·1% 21 640	0·1% 31 808	+1·1
1955	76·8% 34 858 263	100% 26 760 493	49·7% 13 311 936	46·4% 12 404 970	2·7% 722 405	0·9% 225 591	0·1% 33 144	0·2% 62 447	+1·8
1959	78·7% 35 397 080	100% 27 859 241	49·4% 13 749 830	43·8% 12 215 538	5·9% 1 638 571	0·6% 182 708	0·1% 30 897	0·2% 61 619	+1·1
1964	77·1% 35 892 572	100% 27 655 374	43·4% 12 001 396	44·1% 12 205 814	11·2% 3 092 878	0·9% 249 866	0·2% 45 932	0·2% 53 116	−3·1
1966	75·8% 35 964 684	100% 27 263 606	41·9% 11 418 433	47·9% 13 064 951	8·5% 2 327 533	1·2% 315 431	0·2% 62 112	0·3% 75 146	−2·7
1970	72·0% 39 342 013	100% 28 344 798	46·4% 13 145 123	43·0% 12 178 295	7·5% 2 117 033	2·4% 672 356	0·1% 37 970	0·7% 196 019	+4·7
1974 (Feb.)	78·7% 39 798 899	100% 31 333 226	38·2% 11 963 207	37·2% 11 654 726	19·3% 6 063 470	2·6% 803 396	0·1% 32 741	2·6% 815 686	−0·2

†Including all types of Irish Nationalist.

What kinds of people are elected MPs?

House of Commons after 1974 election

a Educational background

	Conservative	Labour
Oxford and Cambridge	162	72
Other universities	37	96
total universities	199	168
Military colleges	10	0
Technical colleges	3	35
Public schools (e.g. Eton, Harrow, Winchester)	198	33
Grammar schools	71	152
Elementary and other secondary schools	7	81

b Occupations

	Conservative	Labour
Barristers and solicitors	66	40
Journalists and publishers	25	24
Teachers and lecturers	7	71
Doctors	2	6
Farmers and landowners	34	1
Company directors	94	6
Accountants	7	3
Insurance underwriters and brokers	16	1
Managers and executives	17	21
Other businessmen	25	22
Engineers	7	24
Clerical and technical workers	2	15
Trade union officials	0	26
Mine workers	0	14
Railway workers	0	6
Other manual workers	0	11
Party officials	3	2
Women MPs	9	13

c Age groupings

	Conservative	Labour
Over 60	31	63
50–59	83	88
40–49	114	94
30–39	53	45
Under 30	3	2

To write, discuss and find out

1 According to opinion polls, a majority of the British people want capital punishment restored. Yet the House of Commons has voted against it. Do you think MPs should echo the views of the people on this issue? Or should they use their own judgment?

2 Why should there be a system of one person —one vote, when people's abilities and interests vary so much?

3 Should voting in elections be made compulsory—as in Australia, where people can be fined for not voting?

4 Can you think of any better ways of selecting party candidates in each constituency?

5 Explain why in 1974 a vote in the Western Isles was four times more valuable than a vote in Daventry.

6 Do you think governments are justified in claiming a *mandate* for policies mentioned in the party manifesto?

7 *Find out* the parliamentary election results in your constituency since World War Two (the reference section of the local library should be helpful) and then answer the following questions:

a what was the total vote for each party at each election, and which party won the seat?

b what was the percentage turnout at each election?

c has the seat ever been 'marginal' during this period?

d has an MP from your constituency held office in a government since 1945?

8 *Find out* about your existing MP, and write a career profile giving details of his or her background, experience, length of service in the Commons and so forth.

9 Listen to a party political broadcast, on radio or TV, from *each* of the major parties. Write comments on:

a *form and content*—what subjects were chosen and how were they handled?

b *effectiveness*—putting aside your own views, which was the most persuasive, and why? Test your reactions on your relatives and friends.

10 What general criticisms would you make of the British electoral system?

Government, prime minister and Cabinet 4

10 Downing Street: the prime minister's official residence in London.

Following a general election, the successful candidate in each constituency becomes a member of the House of Commons. However there is more to an election than the choosing of MPs. People vote mainly for a political party, a party programme and a group of party leaders. The main result of a general election is that a prime minister and a government are chosen by the electorate.

Formation of a government

The prime minister is the most important single person in British government. This is clearly seen immediately after an election. It is his task as the leader of the winning party to pick the members of the Cabinet and government, and allocate work to them. However, as in any form of team selection, the prime minister does not have a completely free hand. Some of the team virtually choose themselves, due to their high standing in the party. A prime minister will want to include in his Cabinet representatives of different shades of opinion, in order to gain maximum support within the party. His main aim must be to create a *balanced* team. As Clement Attlee (Prime Minister, 1945–51) once put it: 'You've got to have a certain number of solid people whom no one would think particularly brilliant, but who between conflicting opinions can . . . give you the ordinary man's point of view.'

If the governing party was in opposition before the election, it will have had a 'Shadow Cabinet' with each member specialising in the work of a government department. Members of a Shadow Cabinet keep an eye on the activities of

The Composition of a Government

Cabinet
Normally 17–24
senior ministers.
Prime minister
is chairman

**Rest of Government
Ministers** of less
important departments,
Junior ministers
(deputies to ministers
in charge of
departments), and
**Parliamentary
secretaries**

Individuals sit on **Cabinet Committees**
responsible for particular areas of policy

Since 1945, prime ministers have lost office only through illness and retirement or election defeat. Although they often become unpopular with some of their MPs and party supporters in the country, no prime minister has lost office because of a party split since 1940 (when Neville Chamberlain was replaced by Winston Churchill).

Both the major parties now elect their leaders by balloting their MPs. In 1963, before this became the practice in the Conservative Party, the Prime Minister was chosen after secret consultations with MPs and Peers. Sir Alec Douglas-Home, then a member of the House of Lords (Lord Home), had to resign his peerage and fight a by-election in order to enter the Commons. This emphasised the now accepted convention that the prime minister must be a member of the Commons. The last premier to sit in the Lords was Lord Salisbury in 1902.

Prime Ministers, 1945–74

Became PM	1945 Labour	1951 Conservative	1955 Conservative	1957 Conservative	1963 Conservative	1964 1974 Labour	1970 Conservative
Prime Minister	**Clement Attlee**	**Winston Churchill** 2nd Premiership: retired before 1955 election	**Anthony Eden** Retired through illness 1957	**Harold Macmillan** Retired through illness 1963	**Sir Alec Douglas-Home**	**Harold Wilson**	**Edward Heath**

Education	Haileybury public school and Oxford University	Harrow public school	Eton public school and Oxford	Eton and Oxford	Eton and Oxford	Wirral Grammar School and Oxford	Chatham House Grammar School and Oxford
Age	62	76	57	62	60	48 57	53

32

government ministers and also present the opposition's alternative policies. Clearly they are in line to run the departments they have specialised in if their party wins power.

In addition to deciding which *individuals* he wants in his Cabinet, the prime minister has to decide which *departments* will be represented there. Some are certainties, such as the Foreign Office or the Treasury, but the inclusion of others will depend on the importance the prime minister attaches to their work. There may be growing responsibilities in some areas of government which justify the promotion of certain departments to Cabinet rank. This has happened in recent years with the Department of Education and Science.

To keep the Cabinet down to a manageable size it is sometimes necessary to combine the work of two or more departments under a single minister. In 1970 this approach allowed Prime Minister Edward Heath to have the smallest Cabinet for some years. As he put it: 'I was determined to have a smaller Cabinet... We've got that . . . We have managed to integrate departments further than ever before, so that we have all the essential fields represented . . . except for aviation and the post office.'

Every Cabinet contains some members who have no special departmental work. These *non-departmental ministers* are vital if the Cabinet is to work smoothly. They can be used to co-ordinate policy between departments, perhaps by chairing small cabinet committees, or they can be given special tasks to perform. When Geoffrey Rippon was Britain's chief negotiator for entry into the EEC (European Economic Community, 1970–72), his official Cabinet position was Chancellor of the Duchy of Lancaster —a purely honorary title. 'I've come to believe that the strength of a Cabinet is in its non-departmental ministers', Harold Wilson once said. 'They are the half-backs of the government team. They don't often score goals or hit the headlines, but no team can be a success without a good half-back line.'

The work of the Cabinet

In normal circumstances the Cabinet meets once or twice a week, in the cabinet room of No. 10 Downing Street. Its main work is to make general decisions on government policy. It does not concern itself with minor details.

Most matters that reach the Cabinet have already been studied in depth by various groups, especially cabinet committees. The exact number and the titles of these committees is usually secret, but it is clear that some are permanent, including those on defence, future legislation and economic policy. Others are set up to deal with more immediate issues, such as prices and incomes or industrial relations. In Harold Wilson's Governments (1964–70) there were about fourteen cabinet committees. Non-cabinet ministers often join these committees if they have specialised knowledge to contribute. So before Cabinet meetings, the circulation of documents, briefings and recommendations will already have taken place. And some members will have attended the earlier preparatory meetings. Consequently decisions can usually be made quite quickly.

If there is a serious disagreement between departments or individual Cabinet members, and the prime minister cannot resolve it himself, it is likely to be discussed in Cabinet. Disputes are fairly common between departments which spend a lot of money and the Treasury, which has to find it. Such disputes are usually settled below Cabinet level—unless the individuals concerned really dig their heels in.

Government policies have to fit together and co-ordinate with each other. For instance, decisions on house building must relate to policies on the use of agricultural land, and work on motorways should not conflict with attempts to preserve the environment. In addition, all governments have a limited amount of money to spend, and must decide their priorities between competing schemes. Should the country have more schools, more hospitals, better pensions, help for regions with high unemployment, or whatever? There is never

Inside the Cabinet Room at 10 Downing Street, London.

enough money to enable everything to be done at once.

So another task of the Cabinet is to co-ordinate policy and decide how resources are to be allocated. Much of this work is done either within departments or in cabinet committees, but the Cabinet carries final responsibility. In arriving at these sorts of decisions the prime minister and non-departmental ministers play a very important part, as they do not have to run complicated departments of their own.

Cabinet meetings

Harold Wilson once talked about Cabinet meetings in an interview:

I've followed very closely what I learned from Attlee when I was a member of his Cabinet: circulation of papers before a meeting; decisions not satisfactorily cleared at department level to be referred to the Prime Minister; extensive use of cabinet committees so that we can economise on the use of the time of the full Cabinet; . . . insistence that all Cabinet reports must have a price tag, meaning that the financial implications must be previously agreed with the Treasury. . . . I also followed Attlee in putting emphasis on the attendance of all members whenever humanly possible, and on punctuality. And the key thing is that when the Cabinet takes a decision, that's it. There was one occasion when I noticed that a new Minister had referred to something that had been decided in Cabinet as a 'proposal'. I sent him a short note saying that the Cabinet makes decisions not proposals, and that was the end of the matter.

Mr Wilson stressed that his Cabinet had, 'talked a good deal less than Clem's (Attlee's) did; did not vote; had got through a good deal of work without bad temper or personal clashes. The committees had been invaluable.' Altogether this extract illustrates some important features of the Cabinet system. Voting is rarely, if ever, used, and it is the prime minister who sums up after discussion and gives the decision of the meeting. This helps to avoid continual and obvious divisions. It also means that the prime minister must be a good chairman. Attlee described it this way:

The job of a prime minister is to get the general feeling, collect the voices. And then when everything reasonable has been said, to get on with the job and say, 'well I think the decision of the Cabinet is this, that or the other. Any objections?' Usually there aren't.

It is a *convention* of British politics that all members of a government accept and defend agreed policy. The unity of a government must always be maintained—at least publicly. There will of course be major arguments in the Cabinet from time to time, but once a policy has been decided each member must accept it or resign. This principle is known as COLLECTIVE CABINET RESPONSIBILITY.

Government has become more complicated in recent years, and the work of a department demands a minister's close attention. Neverthe-less collective responsibility makes it necessary for ministers to keep in touch with the actions of other members of the Cabinet and government, because these might have to be defended publicly. This all helps to create a more unified government, with ministers not narrowly concentrating on their own departments.

How powerful is the prime minister?

From what has been said so far, it is clear that the prime minister has considerable authority in any government. It is his decision when to call a general election, and this gives him the chance to pick a time most favourable for his

In 1962, Prime Minister Harold Macmillan dismissed seven members of his Cabinet in one go—hoping to restore popularity by bringing in younger ministers. The cartoonist Vicky likened him to the Lord High Executioner in the opera The Mikado.

The Conservative Party Conference, October 1970: an ovation for Premier Edward Heath.

own party. He will want policies to be given time to succeed, although he might also bring in popular measures to coincide with an election. The prime minister has the power of appointment to the government—and also the power of dismissal. However this power must be used carefully, to avoid offending important sections of the party.

More than anyone else, the prime minister is at the centre of government. Ministers running departments have little time to step back and take an overall view of policy, whereas it is the prime minister's job to act as supreme co-ordinator in the Cabinet. He has particular responsibilities when there are unexpected crises, disputes between departments or individuals, and decisions to be made on the timing of legislation to be passed through Parliament.

Harold Wilson saw his work as prime minister

in the following way:

The levers of power are all here in No. 10 in the Cabinet Room. The ability of the prime minister to use them depends upon (his) being in touch with what is going on . . . and if all those people around the prime minister—Cabinet officials as well as Cabinet ministers, departmental officials as well as ministers—once realise that the prime minister wants to know what is going on . . . they'll make sure that he gets to know . . . The more they sense that you care, the more they tell you.

The prime minister should be in a position to shape the total strategy of the government. If it lacks one, then he must accept much of the blame. But there is a difference between guiding or encouraging, and interfering. In the past, prime ministers have taken a special interest in certain activities—Eden and Macmillan in foreign affairs, Wilson and Heath in economic

policy. This can mean that ministers in these departments play second fiddle.

The prime minister is the leader of his party both in Parliament and in the country; and can therefore command a great deal of personal loyalty. In the House of Commons he is the government's main spokesman, and twice a week has his own Question Time (see Chapter 7). He is the leader of the nation, and this is emphasised when he performs tasks that are not entirely political: attending receptions, making foreign visits and so on. For many people he *is* the government, and his style of living and personality helps to create an image of the government in the minds of the public. All his activities and characteristics will be examined in the press and on television—and exaggerated by cartoonists.

The government and the party

Despite his great influence, the prime minister is not all powerful. Every Cabinet contains people of considerable importance in the party who are capable of taking over the leadership. Indeed, some of them may be very anxious to do so! No prime minister could force policies through the Cabinet if the majority, or even a powerful minority, were violently opposed to them.

The real centre of power is the prime minister

and the Cabinet, because *together they can control the House of Commons*. Such is the strength of party loyalty and discipline that it is rare for an MP (especially on the government side) to vote against party decisions, or abstain from voting. If a policy is agreed in Cabinet, then it is virtually certain to be accepted by a majority in the House of Commons.

But just as any prime minister has to listen to the views of his Cabinet, so the Cabinet must take into account the feelings, hopes and fears of their MPs. At every level, from official meetings of the party, to informal contact in the dining room, bar or tea rooms in Westminster, members of the government will be anxious to listen to their supporters and explain policies. These same MPs, in turn, will have a similar task to perform with party workers and voters in their constituencies.

On certain issues party loyalty can be severely strained. In the debates on British entry into the EEC, for instance, 'rebel' groups of MPs in both the Conservative and Labour parties voted against their leaders. However, such situations are rare.

Since World War Two, no government has been defeated in the Commons on a *major* issue. But there have been a few near scrapes. No government can afford to take the support of its MPs for granted. And there are a number of other influential groups which the government cannot ignore, including the Press and leaders of big business and the trade unions. The views of these groups, together with the results of by-elections and local elections, help to make the government aware of public reaction to its policies. In the end, the power of the Cabinet depends upon its ability to keep the confidence of both the House of Commons and the country.

To write, discuss and find out

1 Would you expect the following issues to be decided
a within a department,
b in a Cabinet Committee, or
c in full Cabinet?
In each case, give reasons for your choice.
i the prime minister has received an invitation to visit China
ii the Treasury and Ministry of Defence totally disagree about a major item of expenditure
iii the Home Secretary wants to release a man from prison because it is believed he was wrongly convicted
iv a British nuclear submarine has disappeared in the Atlantic
v the Department of Education and Science wants to establish four new universities
vi many government MPs want North Sea gas and oil to be nationalised
2a *Find out* the members of the present Cabinet and the offices they hold (several reference books have this information, including *Whitaker's Almanack*).
b If you were a prime minister picking a cabinet, what factors would you take into account?
3 What is meant by *collective cabinet responsibility?* Does it make for good government, or do you think cabinet ministers should feel free to disagree publicly over policy?
4 'The job of the prime minister is to conduct the orchestra, not to play the instruments himself.' Explain and discuss.
5 If you were an MP on the government side and you had to vote for a new prime minister (on the death or retirement of the previous one) what qualities would you be looking for?
6 Keep a file on the activities of the present prime minister (collect press cuttings, including cartoons, and note the coverage he gets on radio and TV). Compare the publicity the prime minister gets with that given to other members of the Cabinet.

Ministers and departments 5

The wide ranging importance of government in modern society is illustrated simply by looking at the names of the main departments of state. Some departments, and the titles of the ministers in charge, have been in existence for many years. For instance the Treasury (Chancellor of the Exchequer), the Foreign Office (Foreign Secretary), and one or two other ministries date back to the time when govern- ments played a much smaller part in national life. Nowadays governments concern them-

In 1970, Edward Heath merged certain departments and brought them under one minister. The examples given here illustrate the wide range of activities that can be carried on within a single department, and the vast responsibilities of the minister in charge.

Two examples of 'giant' departments

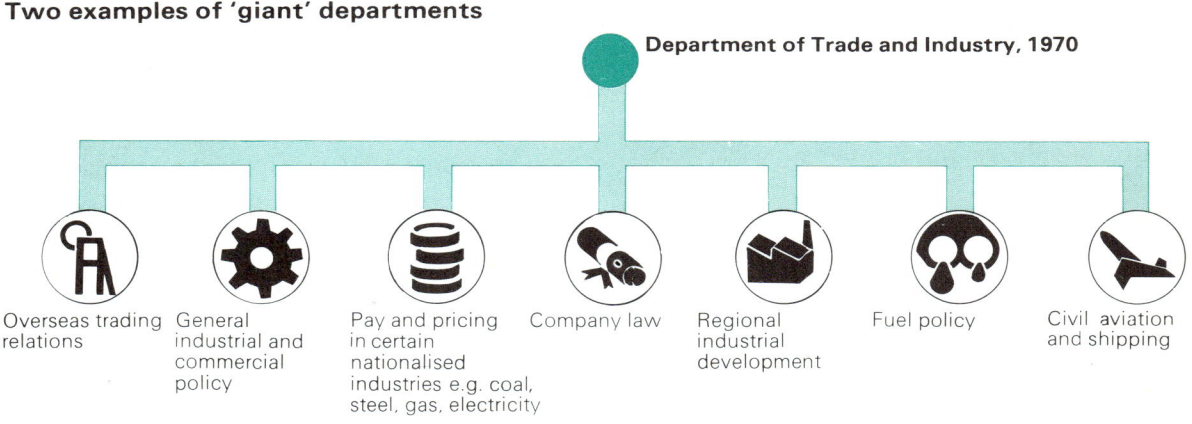

Department of Trade and Industry, 1970

Overseas trading relations | General industrial and commercial policy | Pay and pricing in certain nationalised industries e.g. coal, steel, gas, electricity | Company law | Regional industrial development | Fuel policy | Civil aviation and shipping

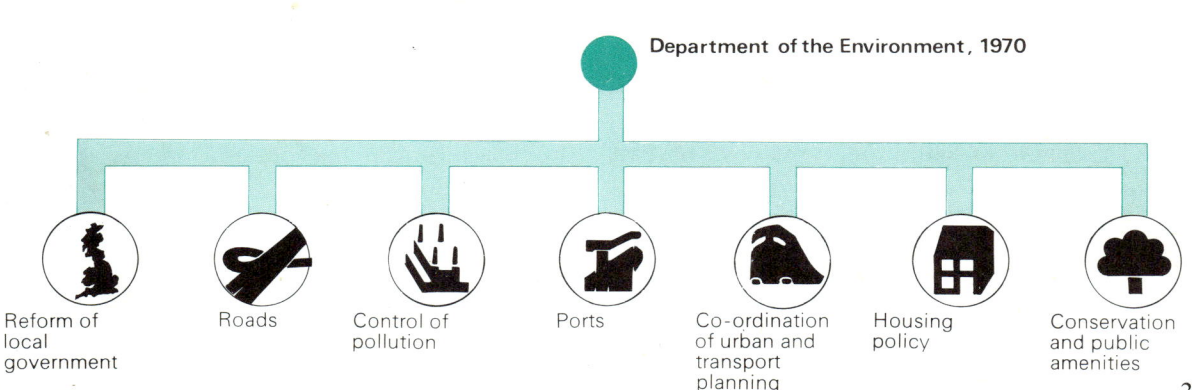

Department of the Environment, 1970

Reform of local government | Roads | Control of pollution | Ports | Co-ordination of urban and transport planning | Housing policy | Conservation and public amenities

selves with a vast range of activities, as is shown by the recent departments that are illustrated on p. 39.

Ministers are important political figures and key administrators as well. In performing these two tasks they lead very busy lives. George Brown, who was Labour Foreign Secretary for a time in the 1960s, once described a typical working day.

Virtually no half hour is unfilled. I was seeing people in the department, receiving visiting statesmen and other groups . . ., attending cabinet committees, and so on. As Deputy Leader of the Party I was, of course, also involved with party work, both in Parliament and outside it. And quite often I would have to be at the House of Commons, either for questions, or to speak in a debate. . . . And so, by the evening, I had already worked a very full day. But round about 6 p.m. the bowler-hatted chaps would start wending their way home, or to their clubs, depositing as they went the papers, the minutes, the telegrams which they thought I should deal with that night. The people in my own office, who of course themselves had already worked a full day, had now to start hours of hectic work, quite unknown in outside industry, in order to 'process' those papers so that I could receive them in relays from then on. I could be pretty sure of enough work to keep me at it until 2 a.m. at least.

The path to office
It is rare for a person to be brought into government at the top level without having served a long apprenticeship in politics. This usually involves some years as an MP in the House of Commons. The normal way of becoming a minister is to gain experience and show ability at the lower levels of government. A reputation for effective speaking in the Commons and general popularity in the party is obviously a help. However, to gain the right sort of experience it is necessary for one's party to gain power from time to time. In October 1964, when Labour returned to power after thirteen years in opposition, there were several top ministers with relatively little experience in government, and some with none at all.

The work of a minister
We shall see that ministers have both political and administrative work (although it is sometimes difficult to separate the two). This is illustrated by looking at the organisation at the top of a major department.

The main task of a minister and his political colleagues is to introduce the values and ideals of the governing party into the work of the department. Civil servants are responsible for day-to-day administration, but they must always take account of the ideals of their political masters. When a change of government occurs, following an election, the Civil Service is expected to work for its new leaders with just the same loyalty and efficiency that it showed under the previous government.

The minister as a politician
Many of the promises contained in the party's election manifesto are put into operation through ministers and their departments. This is particularly true if Acts of Parliament have to be passed. When legislation is under discussion in Parliament, it is the minister and his junior minister who 'steer' it through. They must have a complete mastery of the details of the legislation, which usually comes from careful briefing by civil servants. And they must be certain that the broad aims of the party are being carried out. It is easy for a party to say that it will for example 'encourage regional development', but difficult for a minister to put such a general principle into practice.

The political views of a minister will be reflected in the instructions and recommendations sent out by his department. In 1965 for example the Labour Minister of Education issued a Circular to local education authorities asking them to submit plans for comprehensive education. This had been stated as Labour policy in the 1964 election. The Minister followed up the Circular with speeches, television and radio interviews, conferences, visits around the country and meetings with party workers. In this way he tried to further his political views

Three career profiles

Harold Wilson, born 1916

1945	first elected MP. Parliamentary Secretary to the Minister of Works
1947	President of the Board of Trade (in the Cabinet)
1951	Resigned from the Government
1961	'Shadow' Foreign Secretary
1963	Leader of the Opposition
1964	Prime Minister
1970	Leader of the Opposition
1974	Prime Minister

Harold Wilson's rise to Cabinet rank was very rapid. At the time he was the youngest Cabinet minister since the end of the eighteenth century.

Edward Heath, born 1916

1950	first elected MP
1952	Deputy Chief Whip
1955	Chief Whip
1959	Minister of Labour
1960	Lord Privy Seal
1963	Secretary of State for Industry, Trade and Regional Development
1965	Leader of the Opposition
1970	Prime Minister
1974	Leader of the Opposition

Edward Heath had long experience in government, but only a short time was spent as a minister in charge of a major department.

Roy Jenkins, born 1920

1948	first elected MP
1949 50	Parliamentary Secretary, Commonwealth Relations Office
1964	Minister of Aviation
1965	Home Secretary (in the Cabinet)
1967	Chancellor of the Exchequer
1970	'Shadow' Chancellor and Deputy Leader of the Opposition
1972	Resigned from 'Shadow Cabinet'
1974	Home Secretary

Roy Jenkins had virtually no government experience before 1964, due to Labour's long period in opposition. Yet he rose rapidly to major positions of power.

A Minister and his Department

Cabinet and Cabinet
Committees

Political staff

Civil Service

Junior Ministers
Usually given responsibility for
particular areas within the
department

Minister

Permanent Secretary
Senior civil servant in the
department

**Parliamentary Private
Secretary**
The minister's own choice.
Usually young, and having
his first experience of government

Principal Private Secretary
Although junior in rank, he is
chosen because of his
potential ability. Can become
very close to a minister

To Local Education Authorities
and the Governors of Direct Grant,
Voluntary Aided and Special Agreement Schools

Circular 10/65
12th July, 1965

DEPARTMENT OF EDUCATION AND SCIENCE, CURZON STREET,
LONDON, W.1.

All communications should be addressed to The Permanent Under-Secretary
of State.

THE ORGANISATION OF SECONDARY EDUCATION

I INTRODUCTION

1. It is the Government's declared objective to end selection at eleven plus and
to eliminate separatism in secondary education. The Government's policy has been
endorsed by the House of Commons in a motion passed on 21st January, 1965 :

"That this House, conscious of the need to raise educational standards
at all levels, and regretting that the realisation of this objective is impeded
by the separation of children into different types of secondary schools,
notes with approval the efforts of local authorities to reorganise secondary
education on comprehensive lines which will preserve all that is valuable
in grammar school education for those children who now receive it and
make it available to more children; recognises that the method and timing
of such reorganisation should vary to meet local needs; and believes that
the time is now ripe for a declaration of national policy."

The Secretary of State accordingly requests local education authorities, if they have
not already done so, to prepare and submit to him plans for reorganising secondary
education in their areas on comprehensive lines. The purpose of this Circular is to
provide some central guidance on the methods by which this can be achieved.

II MAIN FORMS OF COMPREHENSIVE ORGANISATION

2. There are a number of ways in which comprehensive education may be
organised. While the essential needs of the children do not vary greatly from one area
to another, the views of individual authorities, the distribution of population and the
nature of existing schools will inevitably dictate different solutions in different areas.
It is important that new schemes build on the foundation of present achievements and
preserve what is best in existing schools.

3. Six main forms of comprehensive organisation have so far emerged from
experience and discussion :

(i) The orthodox comprehensive school with an age range of 11–18.
(ii) A two-tier system whereby *all* pupils transfer at 11 to a junior[1] comprehensive school and *all* go on at 13 or 14 to a senior comprehensive
school.

[1] The terms " junior " and " senior " refer throughout this Circular to the lower and upper
secondary schools in two-tier systems of secondary education.

Left *The Ministry of Education* Circular 10/65,
*which asked local authorities to submit plans for
comprehensive reorganisation. There was no
attempt at compulsion: no law was passed*
forcing *all secondary schools to become
comprehensive.*

as they applied to the Department's work.

It is especially in the House of Commons that
a minister has to prove his political ability. It is
one thing to run a department in the quiet of a
Whitehall office, but quite another to face
questioning and criticism in the Commons. At
Question Time (see Chapter 7) he will be cross-
examined about the actions of his department,
and in full-scale debates he must explain and
defend policy. Such political tasks demand
certain qualities: the ability to speak well, to
translate complicated issues into everyday
language, and to foresee the political effects of
a department's actions.

The minister as an administrator

Because they are politicians, ministers are answerable to the public in a more direct way than civil servants. They accept responsibility for the actions of their officials, through questioning and debate in Parliament. Even though a decision might be relatively unimportant, involving a very junior civil servant, the minister may have to publicly justify what was done. This important convention is known as MINISTERIAL RESPONSIBILITY. It is a safeguard against civil servants using their power in ways that might harm the public. It also means that civil servants are not named in any public controversy.

Another result of ministerial responsibility is what is often called 'red tape'. The phrase has come to mean slowness in making decisions, due to doing everything strictly according to the established rules. But if civil servants' decisions are liable to be publicly investigated, it is not surprising that they are careful to work 'according to the book'. Some slowness in the working of the Civil Service (and this can often be exaggerated), is perhaps a small price to pay for the right of MPs to examine a minister publicly about any of the actions of his officials.

Ministers and civil servants

A minister relies heavily on his civil servants, if only because over 90 per cent of the decisions made in his department never reach him—they are not considered important enough. So civil servants are likely to have far greater knowledge and experience of the detailed work of a department. Besides, politicians tend to be moved around from one department to another, as promotion or demotion occurs in government reshuffles. And for several years at a time they are likely to be out of office altogether.

The fact that ministers have less detailed knowledge of the work of their departments than senior civil servants can often make it difficult for them to give firm leadership. Civil servants are supposed to be politically neutral, but they are bound to have strong views on

Civil servants show they have a sense of humour by calling their magazine Red Tape.

some aspects of policy. So even though the minister is supposed to decide important issues, he will sometimes need great force of personality to go against the advice of his officials.

Two former ministers give surprisingly similar views on the relationship between politicians and civil servants:

The first forty-eight hours decide whether a minister is going to run his office, or whether his office is going to run him. (Arthur Henderson, Labour Foreign Secretary 1929–31)

Ministers can be divided into those who run their departments and those who are run by their departments. I believe Parliament finds out jolly quickly into which category ministers fall, and civil servants know within forty-eight hours of the minister putting his foot over the doorstep. (Iain Macleod, holder of various senior positions in Conservative governments of the late 1950s and early 60s)

Obviously give and take is necessary on both sides. The minister must respect the judgment

Ministerial responsibility

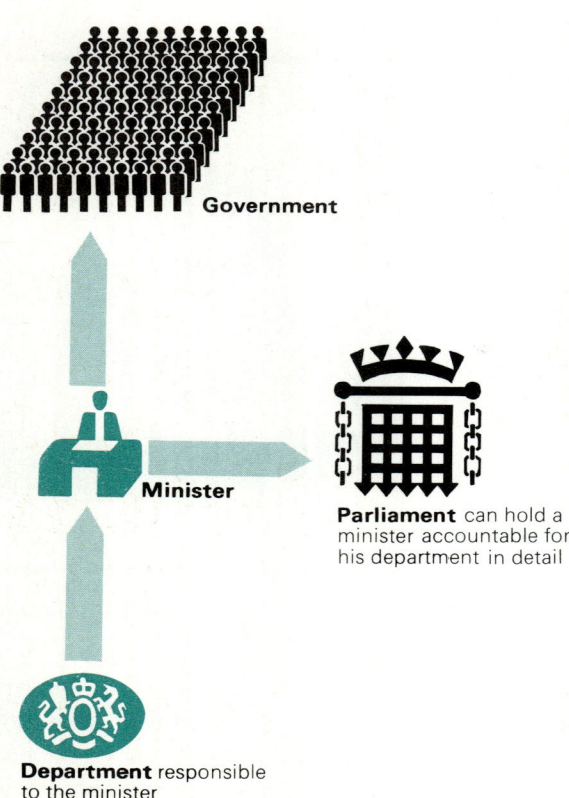

Government

Minister

Parliament can hold a
minister accountable for
his department in detail

Department responsible
to the minister

*A group of Asians, forced to leave Uganda,
arrive at Stansted Airport, September 1972.
The sudden expulsion of Ugandan Asians with
UK passports forced the British government to
decide a policy and act on it very quickly.*

of his civil servants; and they, in turn, must
understand the political responsibility of the
minister to his party. Governments are elected
to carry out certain policies, and where these
affect a department, they must be allowed to
develop. If a government decided to abolish
public schools, then civil servants in the Department of Education and Science would plan
the best way of achieving this, not try to
persuade the minister to drop the scheme.

However some urgent decisions have to be
made in areas where no clear 'party line' has
been established. There might be an unexpected
crisis abroad, such as the expulsion of British
Ugandan Asians in 1972; an industrial dispute,
or a sudden deterioration of the economic
situation. In such cases a minister will be at the
centre of various, and often conflicting, advice;

for the task of civil servants will be to map out
a range of possible policies, and try to estimate
the consequences of each one.

Permanent secretaries

These are the senior civil servants in a department. Because of their important position in
government they can be asked to appear before
committees of the Commons to explain how
public money has been spent. Together with
other top officials in the department, the
permanent secretary will advise the minister on
a variety of matters, including legislation,
speeches and answers to be given to MPs'
questions. So although he represents the top of
the administration of a department, he is also
bound to become involved in the political work
of the minister. Questions such as, 'What will
the opposition say?' or 'Can we keep our own
MPs happy?' will be considered by the minister
and permanent secretary together.

The principle of POLITICAL IMPARTIALITY does
not mean that senior civil servants avoid political
issues entirely. They are expected to respond to

Influences on a Minister

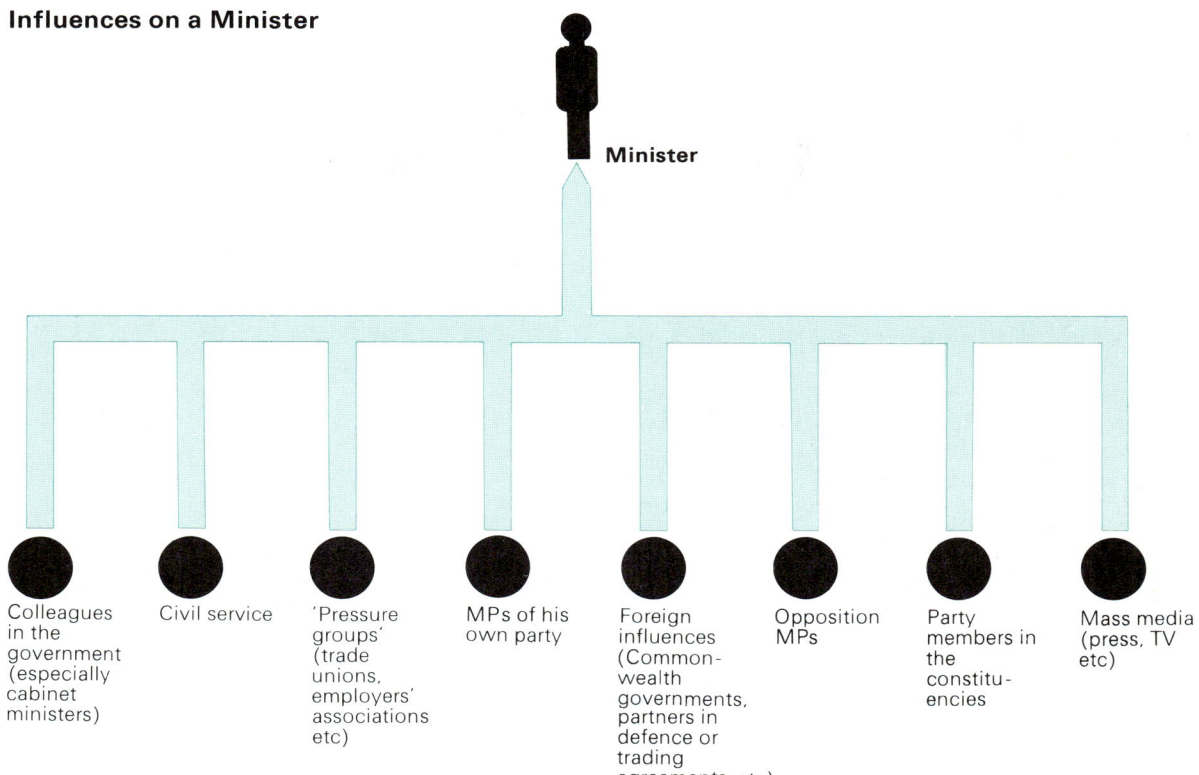

Minister

Colleagues in the government (especially cabinet ministers)

Civil service

'Pressure groups' (trade unions, employers' associations etc)

MPs of his own party

Foreign influences (Commonwealth governments, partners in defence or trading agreements, etc)

Opposition MPs

Party members in the constituencies

Mass media (press, TV etc)

a minister's political views and help him put forward his party policies—whatever party it is. In fact, before an election, talks usually take place between senior civil servants and the main opposition leaders, so that they will be able to work together more easily if the government is defeated.

A minister may lack detailed knowledge of his department's work, and may have limited experience of administering a large organisation. But his duties are different from those of civil servants. He is a political figure, elected into office, who must take public responsibility for the department. He usually has a wealth of political experience to fit him for such a task. As one minister jokingly put it: 'I have no brains myself, I don't need them. Other people have brains, I have judgment.' Another minister once said: 'Political heads of departments are necessary to tell the Civil Service what the public will not stand.'

These pressures and influences are constantly at work. But they are most intense whenever the minister and his department are planning to bring legislation before Parliament. Frequent discussions are held with some of these groups, and others will give their views whether they are asked for them or not.

To write, discuss and find out

1 Some prime ministers have invited business-men, trade unionists and others who are not professional politicians to become senior ministers. What do you think are the advantages and disadvantages of doing this
a for the government;
b from the point of view of the individual concerned?
2 What is meant by *ministerial responsibility*? Is it unfair to a minister in charge of a department?
3 Look back at the diagram showing the structure of the Department of the Environment (1970). Are there any particular areas of responsibility where you think there might be clashes of interest within the Department? Give reasons for your views.
4 What is meant by the *political impartiality* of civil servants? Does it mean that they do not have political views?
5 *Find out* about any three members of the present Cabinet, and write career profiles giving details of their background and experience. How long have they been MPs? How many departments have they served in? How many years did it take them to reach the Cabinet after first entering Parliament?
6 Keep a scrapbook of any important current issue which involves a major government department. In what ways do the minister and his political colleagues try to put their point of view across to the public? What is the attitude of the 'Shadow Minister'? What other individuals or groups in the country have commented on the issue?

A new MP arriving for the first time at the House of Commons must feel a sense of triumph. The highest positions in British politics are normally obtained after a long apprenticeship in the Commons, so he has his foot on the bottom rung of the ladder of political promotion. He may see himself as a future minister, even prime minister, having forgotten how difficult it was to become just an ordinary MP!

A Member of Parliament

After electoral success, our new MP is not without his problems. If he won a marginal

Mr Cyril Smith, a newly elected MP (Liberal, Rochdale), arrives at Westminster to take up his seat, following a by-election, 1972. He has taken the first step on the long and somewhat precarious ladder of political promotion.

seat then he knows that the performance and popularity of his party and its leaders will be vital if he is to even survive the next election. Meanwhile he may have to give up his job, unless it is one that allows scope for part time work—such as journalism or a company

directorship. In any case, he may feel that he should devote all his time to Commons work, and have no outside commitments at all.

As an MP he will have £3250 per year, plus secretarial expenses, free travel to and from his constituency, and free postage and phone calls for official business. However, unless he represents a constituency near London, he may have to run two homes, because most local parties are keen to have their MP living in the area. When Parliament is sitting he may have to work over fourteen hours a day—although five months holiday is some compensation. Many weekends and a large part of the five month holiday will be spent in his constituency.

A good deal of an MP's time is spent obtaining information and sorting out problems for constituents, as well as on his own research for

MPs like Jo Grimond (Liberal, Orkney and Zetland—pictured here) have to do a lot of costly and time-consuming travelling in order to visit their constituencies.

speeches, articles, and so forth. It is important for MPs to be well informed if they are to be effective in examining the actions of government or explaining their party policy. The vast majority of MPs are extremely conscientious in carrying out the variety of tasks which their work involves. There are times when it is popular to belittle the politician—and no doubt this is a healthier attitude than one of exaggerated respect. But we should not forget that the MP represents one of the most powerful defences against unfair and unjust actions by the state.

The chamber of the House

The old House of Commons was destroyed in an air raid in 1941. Consequently the main features of the present Chamber were deliberately planned when it was rebuilt after the war. Some people say that the very size and shape of the Chamber, and the procedure used in the Commons, influences the way in which the political system works. For instance the Chamber is surprisingly small. There is not enough room to seat all MPs on the benches at any one time. This is rarely a problem, however,

The French National Assembly. As in most European parliaments, its members sit in a semi-circle: on the left, 'social reform' parties; on the right, parties opposing rapid change. Hence the political terms left- and right-wing.

The House of Commons

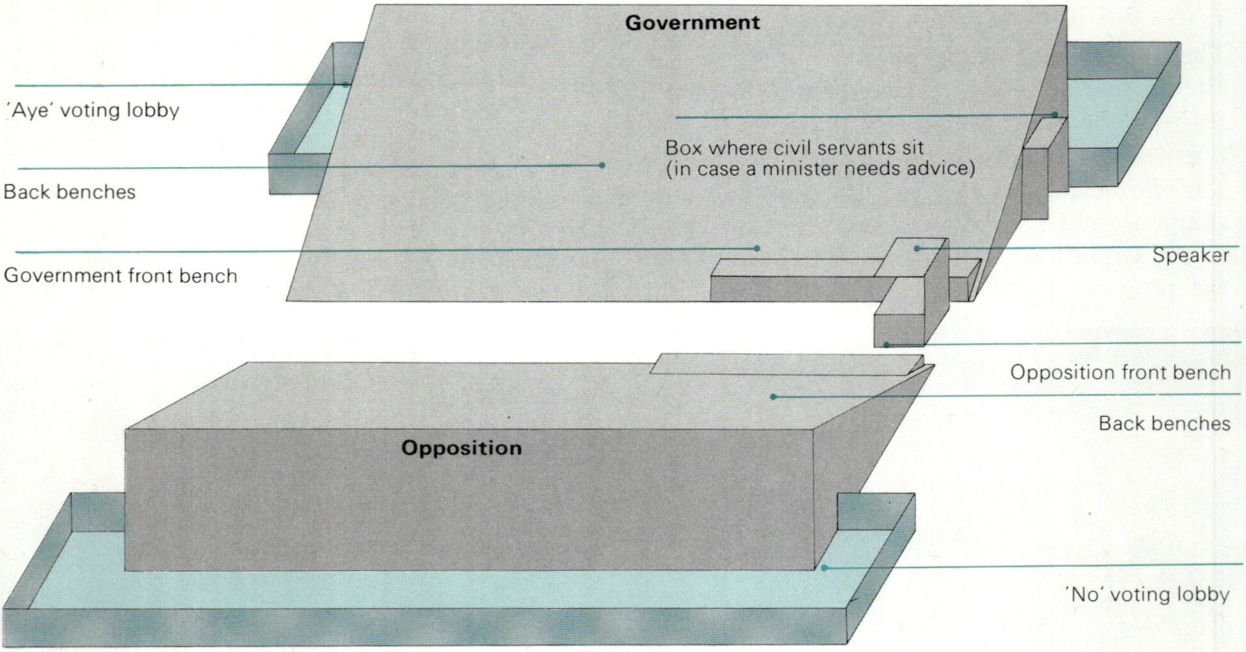

Government

'Aye' voting lobby

Back benches

Government front bench

Box where civil servants sit
(in case a minister needs advice)

Speaker

Opposition front bench

Back benches

Opposition

'No' voting lobby

since a 'full house' is unusual. The great advantage of having a small Chamber is that it allows a relaxed, almost conversational style of speaking. And on important occasions, when there is a good attendance, it produces a sense of packed excitement.

MPs do not speak from a rostrum at the front—unlike elected representatives in many foreign parliaments. They merely stand up, once they have been called by the Speaker. It is generally felt that a rostrum encourages an emotional style of speaking, and makes it difficult for members to interrupt. When MPs vote, they walk into one of the two lobbies ('Aye' or 'No') and are counted as they emerge through a type of gate. Perhaps this helps to cool tempers after a hectic debate!

The main government and opposition leaders sit on the front benches facing each other. Consequently the phrase 'back-bench MPs' refers to Members who do not hold any official post, and therefore sit on the benches at the back. The rectangular shape of the Commons certainly gives a strong impression of the government and opposition being engaged in conflict; and, more important, it emphasizes the idea of the opposition being an alternative government. The members of the Shadow Cabinet speak from their own front bench, and there is an obvious alternative prime minister in the *leader of the opposition* (leader of the second largest party).

The chairman in the Commons is the *Speaker*, who is chosen from among the MPs themselves, usually by agreement between the main parties. On becoming Speaker he must be politically impartial, for he has complete control of procedure in the House. Together with his deputies, he has the daunting task of listening to everything that is said! All speeches are published daily in *Hansard*, which is a record of the proceedings of the Commons.

Outside the main chamber of the Commons are other lobbies, where for example MPs can meet members of the general public. The practice of confronting MPs about grievances or in favour of particular policies is in fact known as *lobbying*. The main chamber of the House is of course the real focus of political activity. However a great deal of work, especially in the various committees of the Commons, takes place 'upstairs' (outside the chamber).

Political parties in the Commons

Political parties run like a thread through this book. In Chapter 1 they were described as special sorts of groups which exist to obtain power. In Chapter 3 we saw that they are central to British elections, because the overwhelming majority of people vote on a party basis. Parties simplify issues, and give voters a clear choice between alternative policies. Because MPs owe their position to their party label almost all of them vote according to the 'party line'.

Supporting the party is a particularly important responsibility for government MPs. Although the prime minister and Cabinet are the most powerful people in British politics, this is only because they can always command a majority in the Commons. If they lose this majority, in a vote on a major issue of policy, then they may well have to resign. From this it follows that party organisation in the Commons is vital for the survival of a government. Political parties are examined in detail in Chapter 11. Meanwhile in this chapter we shall look at the part they play in the Commons.

The emergence of political parties as we know them today was largely due to the extension of the right to vote in the nineteenth and early twentieth centuries. Once voters numbered millions rather than thousands, it was necessary for the earlier, more loosely knit groups in Parliament to organise themselves on a national scale. To get enough support to win control of the Commons, candidates standing for a clear party policy had to be put up in every constituency.

But winning a party majority in the Commons is only a first step. A ruling party has to have ways of *keeping* control, so that the government

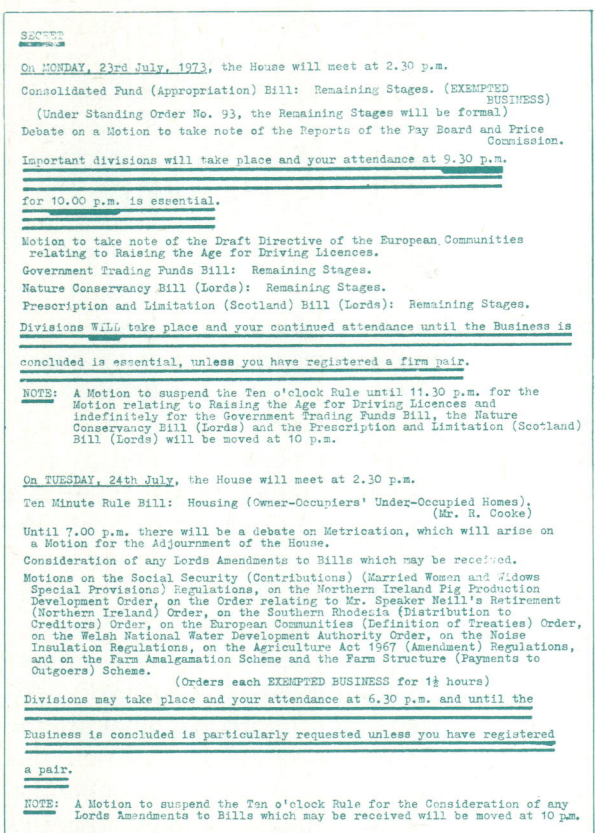

SECRET

On MONDAY, 23rd July, 1973, the House will meet at 2.30 p.m.

Consolidated Fund (Appropriation) Bill: Remaining Stages. (EXEMPTED BUSINESS)
(Under Standing Order No. 93, the Remaining Stages will be formal)
Debate on a Motion to take note of the Reports of the Pay Board and Price Commission.

Important divisions will take place and your attendance at 9.30 p.m.

for 10.00 p.m. is essential.

Motion to take note of the Draft Directive of the European Communities relating to Raising the Age for Driving Licences.
Government Trading Funds Bill: Remaining Stages.
Nature Conservancy Bill (Lords): Remaining Stages.
Prescription and Limitation (Scotland) Bill (Lords): Remaining Stages.

Divisions WiLL take place and your continued attendance until the Business is

concluded is essential, unless you have registered a firm pair.

NOTE: A Motion to suspend the Ten o'clock Rule until 11.30 p.m. for the Motion relating to Raising the Age for Driving Licences and indefinitely for the Government Trading Funds Bill, the Nature Conservancy Bill (Lords) and the Prescription and Limitation (Scotland) Bill (Lords) will be moved at 10 p.m.

On TUESDAY, 24th July, the House will meet at 2.30 p.m.

Ten Minute Rule Bill: Housing (Owner-Occupiers' Under-Occupied Homes). (Mr. R. Cooke)

Until 7.00 p.m. there will be a debate on Metrication, which will arise on a Motion for the Adjournment of the House.
Consideration of any Lords Amendments to Bills which may be received.
Motions on the Social Security (Contributions) (Married Women and Widows Special Provisions) Regulations, on the Northern Ireland Pig Production Development Order, on the Order relating to Mr. Speaker Neill's Retirement (Northern Ireland) Order, on the Southern Rhodesia (Distribution to Creditors) Order, on the European Communities (Definition of Treaties) Order, on the Welsh National Water Development Authority Order, on the Noise Insulation Regulations, on the Agriculture Act 1967 (Amendment) Regulations, and on the Farm Amalgamation Scheme and the Farm Structure (Payments to Outgoers) Scheme.
(Orders each EXEMPTED BUSINESS for 1½ hours)
Divisions may take place and your attendance at 6.30 p.m. and until the

Business is concluded is particularly requested unless you have registered

a pair.

NOTE: A Motion to suspend the Ten o'clock Rule for the Consideration of any Lords Amendments to Bills which may be received will be moved at 10 p.m.

can always command support on major issues. How is this done?

Party organisation

Each political party has certain MPs called *whips*, who control day-to-day organisation in the Commons. The name comes from a hunting expression (whipping in), but although it sounds fierce and disciplinary, MPs are not in fact bullied into supporting their parties. The vast majority of MPs would do so freely, whips or no whips. Their belief in their party and its policies, coupled with a reluctance to 'rock the boat' and cause disunity, will usually ensure their support. MPs are only likely to threaten to abstain or vote against their party on particularly controversial issues, and even then the numbers involved are small.

The main task of the whips is to send out details of forthcoming business to their MPs, and to ensure that the party votes at its maxi-

mum strength on important debates. If an MP cannot be in the Commons to record his vote, perhaps because he is in his constituency, then his party whips will try to get him 'paired' with an MP on the other side. This means the rival whips agree that neither MP will vote; thus keeping the relative strengths of the parties equal. A more general responsibility of the whips is to keep their party leaders in touch with the views of back-benchers. As a former cabinet minister, Lord Hill, put it: 'A (government) Chief Whip's job is to listen and learn, to gather up the scraps of gossip, to assess other people's opinions. He is the prime minister's ears and eyes in the smoking room and in the lobby.'

Although political parties are firmly united on most issues, they do nevertheless contain groups with differing opinions. Every now and again some back-benchers will be unhappy with official party policy—or even severely critical of it—and then it is the job of the whips to try to prevent a split. Friendly persuasion is likely to be more effective than threats or bullying, and the most severe threat of all—expulsion from the parliamentary party—is avoided if at all possible.

If a revolt by government MPs against the party leadership cannot be prevented, its seriousness will depend on the size of both the rebel group and the government's majority in the House. When a government has a tiny majority, as it did under Labour from October 1964 to March 1966, even a handful of rebel MPs can threaten it with disaster. However in such cases there is tremendous pressure on the rebels not to embarrass the government. If a ruling party were forced to go into a general election while its ranks were split, many of its MPs would be in danger of losing their seats.

Party meetings

These are held regularly and, because they are private, MPs express their views frankly. Meetings of government MPs are often addressed by ministers, who on controversial issues can face sharp criticism. But it does not follow that these meetings decide policy. That is largely the job of party leaders; although they must obviously take account of what is generally acceptable.

Party meetings allow leaders to assess the views of back-bench MPs, and everyone has a chance to let off steam. But because they are private they do nothing to assist public understanding of government. The desire to keep up a public image of party unity means that some of the fiercest and best argued debates in Westminster take place behind closed doors.

In the end, unity is maintained simply because no party can do without it. To win power, or keep it, is the main aim of parties and their leaders. And public arguments and splits within a party can ruin its chances of winning the next general election.

The opposition

A basic task of the opposition is to examine government decisions critically and provide a check on any misuse of power. It is true that some party battles in the Commons, in which the opposition objects to practically everything the government does, seem petty and trivial. But it is the responsibility of the opposition to ensure that as many objections as possible are put forward and discussed before the government goes ahead with its policy.

Criticism for its own sake, however, is not enough. The leader of the opposition and his Shadow Cabinet are the alternative government. They are expected to be constructive and put forward positive policies of their own. The electorate cannot be expected to trust them with office in the future unless they give the impression of being able to run the country.

Left *Details of forthcoming Commons business sent out by a party Whip. The underlinings show the importance of each topic.*
Right *Anthony Eden (top), Aneurin Bevan (centre) and Iain Macleod. At various times all had serious disagreements with their parties, yet retained their political influence.*

Sydney Silverman, MP was a sponsor of the Bill to end capital punishment in 1965. The Bill was carried on a free vote—*it would have been senseless to have made a party issue out of a matter of conscience like this.*

In the day-to-day business of the House, opposition arguments may appear to have little or no effect. The voting of MPs is rarely in any doubt, and at the end of every major debate the government will almost certainly win. Does this make debates a sham—rather like watching a football match when the result has been decided beforehand? Not really, because the main purpose of party battles in the Commons is to force the government to explain and defend its actions. This is an old Commons tradition, dating back to the days when the government was the monarch. Today it is largely the task of the opposition rather than the Commons as a whole, although a government's own MPs do offer criticism at closed party meetings.

Many people would like to see MPs vote less frequently along party lines. At present this only happens when there is a *free vote*—usually on such issues as divorce, abortion, capital punishment or licensing laws, where party labels would be objectionable. Should free votes be extended to more politically controversial areas? If they were (and if MPs really did become less willing to support their parties, which is by no means certain) then government as we know it might become unworkable. The present near-certainty of voting in the Commons does at least make governments secure enough to carry out a full political programme.

To write, discuss and find out

1 Turn back to the list of occupations of MPs at the end of Chapter 3. Which of these could be continued on a part-time basis after election to Parliament and which could not? Do you think it right for an MP to have commitments outside politics?

2 Why are strongly organised parties considered important to the working of the House of Commons?

3 Can you name any present MPs who are firmly opposed to one or more of their *own* party's policies? Give details, and try to find out if they are supported by their constituency parties.

4 If you were a chief whip, what arguments might you use to persuade a 'rebel' MP to vote with the party?

5 What opportunities do MPs have for voicing disagreement with their own party leaders or policies? When are such complaints likely to be most effective?

6 'The opposition just disagrees with the government for the sake of argument and stops it getting on with the work it was elected to do.' What are the arguments against this view?

7 *Find out* about the present Speaker of the Commons: his political background, his present constituency (and majority), how long he has held the office, where he lives, the salary he is paid, and so on. (Again, reference books such as *Whitaker's Almanack* should be consulted.)

The Commons at work

7

A large part of this chapter is given to expanding this diagram of the main areas of Commons activity.

Much of the legislation (law making) is concerned with the political promises made by the government in its election manifesto. However, as we shall see, not all legislation is sponsored by the government. Control of finance is different. Only the government is allowed to put forward proposals for raising money by taxation, although it must always obtain Commons' approval. Government spending is now so vast that a really close examination of finance is very difficult. Part of this work is done 'upstairs', by committees of the Commons.

Debates on policy may be introduced either by the government or the opposition. They are generally concerned with the broad outlines of policy rather than matters of detail. Finally, some time is spent examining the administration (carrying out) of government decisions, especially through the Civil Service. Here MPs expect efficiency, together with justice for groups and individuals (including their own constituents) who are affected by government decisions.

Legislation

Apart from Bills to put into effect its political promises, a government will find it necessary to introduce other legislation. There may be a need to tidy up existing laws; an unexpected crisis may occur, or civil servants may persuade their ministers that certain legal changes are desirable. On some of these issues the opposition will back the government, as sometimes happens when a threat to British interests abroad calls for swift legislation. But whether there is agreement or not, all *Public Bills* (sponsored by the government) are carefully examined. They take up the bulk of Commons' time spent on legislation.

Private Bills usually deal with the powers of local authorities. They may be of great interest to certain regions of the country, but rarely

Allocation of time in the Commons

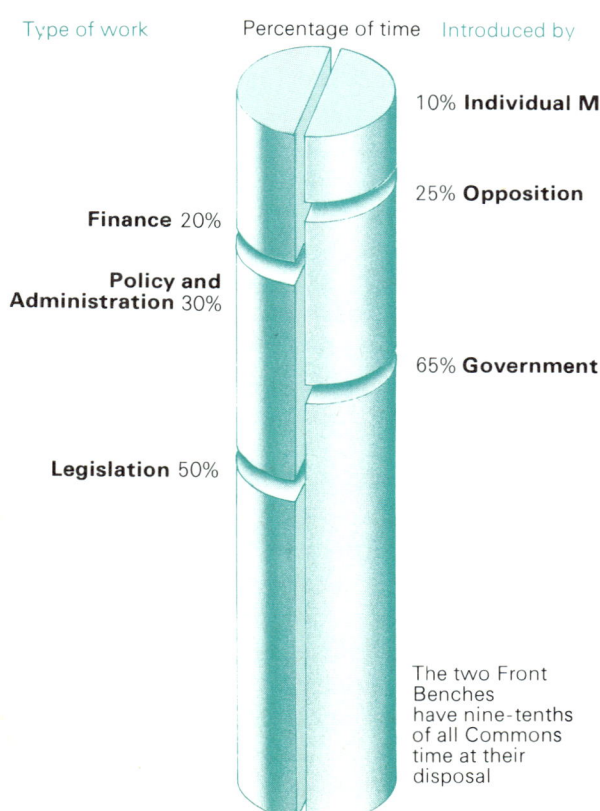

Type of work

Percentage of time   Introduced by

10% **Individual MPs**

25% **Opposition**

Finance 20%

Policy and Administration 30%

65% **Government**

Legislation 50%

The two Front Benches have nine-tenths of all Commons time at their disposal

Types of Bills

Public Bills — Sponsored by the Government, and consequently almost certain to be passed.

Private Bills — Usually sponsored by local authorities (councils) who want to add to their powers.

Private Members' Bills — A ballot is held to select the 'lucky' MPs who can present Bills. These are only likely to succeed if the government is not against them.

When legislation is passing through Parliament it is called a Bill. It becomes an Act of Parliament when it has been agreed to by the Commons and the Lords and signed by the Monarch. It is then the law of the land.

have any national importance. Much of the detailed committee work on these Bills is done by the House of Lords (see Chapter 8).

Back-bench MPs are normally given about twenty Fridays in each session of 160 days to to introduce *Private Members' Bills*. Most of these Bills do not become Acts of Parliament, but they at least give MPs a chance to air grievances, or to show a need for legislation. If a Bill is supported by a large number of MPs, and especially by the government, it does stand a good chance of succeeding. Occasionally the government will prefer to have an issue considered through this kind of Bill and will give extra time to it. For instance in recent years changes in the laws affecting abortion, divorce and capital punishment have taken place through Private Members' Bills.

How are laws passed?

Before a Bill is presented to Parliament a great deal of preliminary work has to be done. It must make legal sense, and be carefully worded so as to avoid 'loopholes'. Consultations with individuals and groups most directly concerned are a necessary first stage. Prior to Public Bills, the government sometimes issues 'green papers', which put forward ideas to be discussed, or 'white papers', which give rather more concrete proposals.

So well before a Bill is finalised the government will have a fairly clear idea of opinions and reactions towards it. At some stage a government sponsored Bill goes before a cabinet committee; and then, for final approval, to the Cabinet itself. During this time the Bill will be drafted into a clear and definite form, with the help of government legal departments.

Procedure in Parliament

Bills can first be presented to either the Commons or the Lords, after which they go through the same procedure. The passing of Bills is a lengthy and complicated business. No doubt it could be streamlined by using smaller and more expert committees, and by taking the Second and Third Readings in committee rather than in the Commons itself. But it is believed that speed and efficiency should be sacrificed in

Two successful sponsors of Private Members' Bills: David Steel (left) who fought to legalise abortion in certain cases, and Leo Abse (above) who presented a Bill to reform the law on homosexual practices.

order to give the Commons the fullest opportunity to examine Bills publicly.

Control of finance

Directly or indirectly, the government is responsible for spending well over £20,000 million every year. How this money should be spent is obviously a matter of great importance to the Commons, and there are many debates about priorities. For instance, should more money go to education, the social services or defence? Most people will have their own preferences. And the same applies to the ways in which governments *raise* money—mainly through borrowing and taxation—except that the usual cry is for there to be less taxation!

Only the government can propose the raising and spending of money. But in order to do this they must have the permission of the Commons. This is an ancient Commons privilege, going back to the Middle Ages, when members would grant money to the monarch on condition that

Stages of a Bill passing through Parliament

First Reading

No debate — The title of the Bill is read out, and printed copies made available so that MPs can study the proposals

Second Reading

Debate on general principles. Usually takes place in the Commons, but can be in committee — Bill is either rejected or (as is almost certain if sponsored by the government) accepted

Committee Stage

Bill is examined in detail and amendments can be made. This is the vital stage for the minister or junior ministers in charge of the Bill — There are six regular or 'standing' committees. Between 25 and 40 MPs will be involved at this stage (in proportion to party strength in the Commons). These MPs sometimes have a specialist interest in the subject, and the changes in the Bill that they propose are often accepted by the government. Some important Bills are considered by a Committee of the Whole House, in the main Commons chamber

Report Stage

The amended Bill is 'reported' to the Commons. It can go directly to the Third Reading

Third Reading

A debate, similar to the Second Reading. But it need not be held.

The Bill then goes to the Lords (or to the Commons if it started in the Lords) and through similar stages. If there is a conflict between the two Houses, then the Bill must take the form decided on by the Commons — although the Lords can delay it for up to a year.

Royal Assent

Now automatic — a *convention* — In theory the Monarch can refuse to sign the Bill, but this has not happened since 1707. If the Monarch refused, it would bring the Crown directly into politics and threaten its independence — and survival

Finance

A
BILL
INTITULED

An Act to grant certain duties, to alter other duties, and to amend the law relating to the National Debt and the Public Revenue, and to make further provision in connection with Finance.

Brought from the Commons 12*th July* 1973

Ordered to be printed 12th July 1973

LONDON
Printed and published by
Her Majesty's Stationery Office
Printed in England at St Stephen's
Parliamentary Press

68p net

they were allowed to express their grievances. Today, the problem facing the Commons is not so much to be able to express grievances, but to keep some hold over the vast area of government expenditure. It is not possible for the whole House to examine in detail how all the money is spent.

Every year the *Finance Bill* contains the main proposals for government expenditure. Once passed, it gives the government authority to raise the money it needs. Most of the work on this Bill is done 'upstairs' in committee, although three days of Commons' time are used by the opposition to debate selected items from the Bill.

The main Commons control of finance is carried out by two committees: the *Select Committee on Expenditure* and the *Public Accounts Committee*. Each year the government publishes its estimates of spending—filling hundreds of closely typed pages—and the Expenditure Committee examines them and tries to discover how efficiently departments are run. The Committee has its own research staff and can call civil servants in as witnesses. The Public Accounts Committee also has its own staff. Its main work is to examine government accounts, to see if value for money has been obtained. Although the Committee tends to work a few years behind, it does provide a further check on financial mismanagement.

Debates on major issues

Many debates in the Commons are directly connected with the passing of Bills. However at frequent intervals more general debates are held in which the government explains its policies and the opposition is able to criticise them. Many of these debates are introduced by the government, but on twenty-nine days of the year the opposition can choose the subject. The range of topics is vast and will include foreign affairs, social policy, education, defence and the urgent issues of the time.

Commons debates are given great publicity in the press and on radio and television. For this reason the floor of the Commons is one of the best places from which to speak to the nation.

The work of individual MPs

Ninety per cent of Commons' time is taken up with work introduced by government and opposition leaders. Nevertheless there are certain occasions when the individual MP comes into his own.

Question Time

Four days a week, ministers have to answer questions put to them by MPs on both sides. The prime minister has two days, and the rest of the time is divided between departmental ministers on a rota basis. Ministers can only be

Question time in the Commons

Breakdown of questions in a typical week

	Written answers	Oral answers
Monday	118	31
Tuesday	132	33
Wednesday	116	34
Thursday	74	38
Friday	54	—

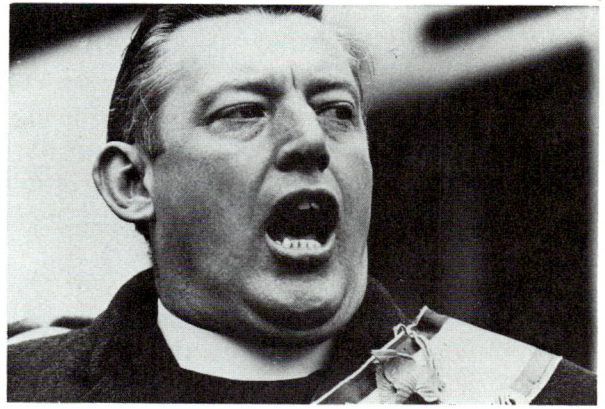

Types of questions (taken from records for July 1971)

Mr Elystan Morgan asked the Prime Minister what steps he intends to take during the Summer Recess to explain to the people of Wales what is involved in Britain's entry into the European Economic Community?

Rev. Ian Paisley asked the Minister of State for Defence under what circumstances the army was called to an electricity transformer in McClure Street, Belfast, on or about 17 July, after an IRA bomb explosion; what time the explosion took place; what time the army arrived; what was the result of the investigations; how the bomb was detonated; what amount of damage was done; whether the area was sealed off; what searches were made, and what arrests resulted?

Mr O'Halloran asked the Secretary of State for Education and Science when she proposes to announce her decision on the rebuilding of Grafton School, London N7, and on the provision of a new Roman Catholic school in Elthorne Road, London N19?

Mr Milne asked the Secretary of State for Education and Science if she will publish a list of the new schools built in Northumberland during the past ten years?

Mr Arthur Lewis asked the Secretary of State for Trade and Industry whether he has received the communication from the Hon. Member for West Ham, North, enclosing a letter from an accountant making charges against a public company and complaints against his Department?

Sir R Russell asked the Secretary of State for Foreign and Commonwealth Affairs how many refugees have sought protection in Hong Kong after escaping from the People's Republic of China in each year since 1949?

questioned about activities over which they have a direct responsibility. However because of the principle of *ministerial responsibility* (see Chapter 5) the whole range of a department's work can usually be included. This means that Question Time is important for investigating the actions of civil servants, especially in their dealings with the public.

Questions may be asked for a variety of reasons: to embarrass the government, to obtain information, to press for action on an issue, and so forth. Sometimes innocent looking questions are followed up with *supplementary* (additional) questions which catch the minister unprepared! Departments take all questions very seriously, even those calling for a written answer (which are not therefore raised orally in the Commons). Question Time illustrates two of the most important tasks of MPs—to keep a watchful eye on the government and to protect the rights of individuals.

Adjournment debates

These are held at the end of every day and last for half an hour. An ordinary MP (selected some time before by ballot) introduces the subject for debate, and the minister responsible for that particular area of government replies. Adjournment debates give MPs a chance to develop their arguments in some detail. Their reasons for picking topics can be as varied as those for asking questions, and local constituency matters are often chosen.

Constituency problems

Assuming that an MP is fairly conscientious, the main bulk of his work is likely to arise in the constituency. Most MPs hold regular 'surgeries', to which constituents come with their problems —some to do with government departments, others involving local councils, private companies and so on. It is a measure of the influence of MPs that letters they write on behalf of constituents in such matters often produce rapid results. No doubt this is partly due to the fact that MPs can, if necessary, ask questions

---

A week in the Commons (in July 1971)

Monday
Question time
Statement on the economic situation by the Chancellor of the Exchequer
Statement on the European Economic Community by the Leader of the House
Debate on a Government White Paper on housing
Adjournment debate: river pollution in south-east Lancashire

Tuesday
Question Time – the Prime Minister
Debate on economic affairs, introduced by the Government
Adjournment debate: Icelandic fishing limits

Wednesday
Question Time
Statement on the dumping of waste into the Atlantic
Debate on entry into European Economic Community (Government White Paper)
Adjournment debate: dismissal of a college lecturer

Thursday
Question Time
Statement on the hijacking of a BOAC aeroplane
Debate on entry into European Economic Community (Government White Paper)
Adjournment debate: selling paintings to overseas buyers

Friday
Debate on entry into European Economic Community (Government White Paper)
Adjournment debate: secondary education in Bexley

In this particular week the debate on entry into the European Economic Community overshadowed everything else—even to the extent of making Friday (often a 'quiet' day) very important in the Commons week. The Adjournment debates provide opportunities to discuss matters arising in particular constituencies.

Issues raised in one weekly 'surgery' in a Midlands constituency, 1972

	Issue	Action taken by MP
Housing	Two requests for places in old people's bungalows	
	Young couple living with parents in overcrowded house want council flat	Letters sent to local council's housing manager. Some put in touch with a local councillor
	Middle aged couple in damp council house want transfer	
	Crippled woman with small child wants ground floor flat	
Pensions and superannuation	Two want an increase in pensions for the disabled	Letters to Health Service Superannuation Division
	Two men worried about redundancy scheme for miners	Letter to Department of Health and Social Security
	Widow of a man who died after a pit accident believes she is not receiving enough Social Security	Letter to Department of Health and Social Security
	War widow angry because two-thirds of her pension goes back in tax — the result, she claims, of working to support her sons	Letter to the Chancellor of the Exchequer
Other problems	Complaint about interference on a television set caused by a local amateur radio operator	Letter to local GPO Manager
	Presentation of a petition to put a footpath through part of a local village. Letters sent seven years ago to the county council not answered	Petition accepted and sent to the county council with the MP's support
	Mother claims that her daughter, sent to a home for maladjusted children, is not allowed to see her. The girl is now pregnant	Letter sent to the Children's Home

During the same 'surgery' two people called to thank the MP for his efforts in the past — one had got back a lost sewing machine, and the other had been granted a transfer of council houses. In this particular constituency the MP always writes the necessary letters while the people concerned are present. And he has a member of the local council with him, to help sort out local issues, especially housing.

It has to be admitted that not all MPs are as conscientious as they should be in their constituency work, and some do not actively encourage their constituents to see them. But the vast majority of MPs consider the protection of the rights of constituents to be a central part of their work.

Dick Taverne, MP, became a victim of 'conflicting loyalties' when his view of the national interest clashed with the policy of his Constituency Labour Party in Lincoln.

in the Commons and cause unwelcome publicity.

In all his constituency work, an MP's main responsibility is to protect people's rights under the law. Many laws are very complicated, and individuals often have the utmost difficulty in picking their way through the complications of welfare benefits, social security payments, housing legislation and so on. MPs are well equipped to give advice on such matters.

Conflicting loyalties

An MP's natural loyalties to both his parliamentary party and his constituency can sometimes conflict. For instance party policy on such

matters as the closure of unprofitable railways or coal mines may clash with the interests of his constituents. Many other sorts of conflicting loyalties can arise in the day-to-day work of an MP. Let us consider same examples.

As a politician, an MP will have firm views about what his party stands for; and on some occasions he may think that the party leaders are not sticking to these principles. This is perhaps most likely to happen where MPs are strongly attached to outside pressure groups, such as trade unions. In the late 1960s Harold Wilson's Labour Government was forced to drop planned legislation affecting trade unions largely because of the opposition of union-sponsored Labour MPs.

Another possible cause of conflict for an MP is his need to keep the support of his constituency party. In the early 1970s Dick Taverne, Labour MP for Lincoln, lost this support due to his views on a number of issues, including British entry to the EEC. He resigned and fought a by-election (1973) in which he defeated the local party's official candidate. As we saw in Chapter 3, S. O. Davies did much the same thing in Merthyr Tydfil in the general election of 1970. But others have been less fortunate. In 1956 Nigel Nicholson, Conservative MP for Bournemouth, opposed his government's action in invading the Suez Canal Zone of Egypt. He was not supported by his constituency party, who chose another candidate for the next election, and Nicholson lost his seat.

This is an example of a conflict between party loyalty and what an MP considers to be in the 'national interest'. It happened on a large scale during the debates over British entry into the EEC (1971–72). A number of MPs on both sides voted against their party leadership because they felt that the 'national interest' was at stake. Similarly in 1940, when the war was going badly, a number of Conservative MPs refused to support the prime minister, Neville Chamberlain. Although he won a vital Commons vote (on the British withdrawal from Norway), it was clear that he could not

The Loyalties of an MP

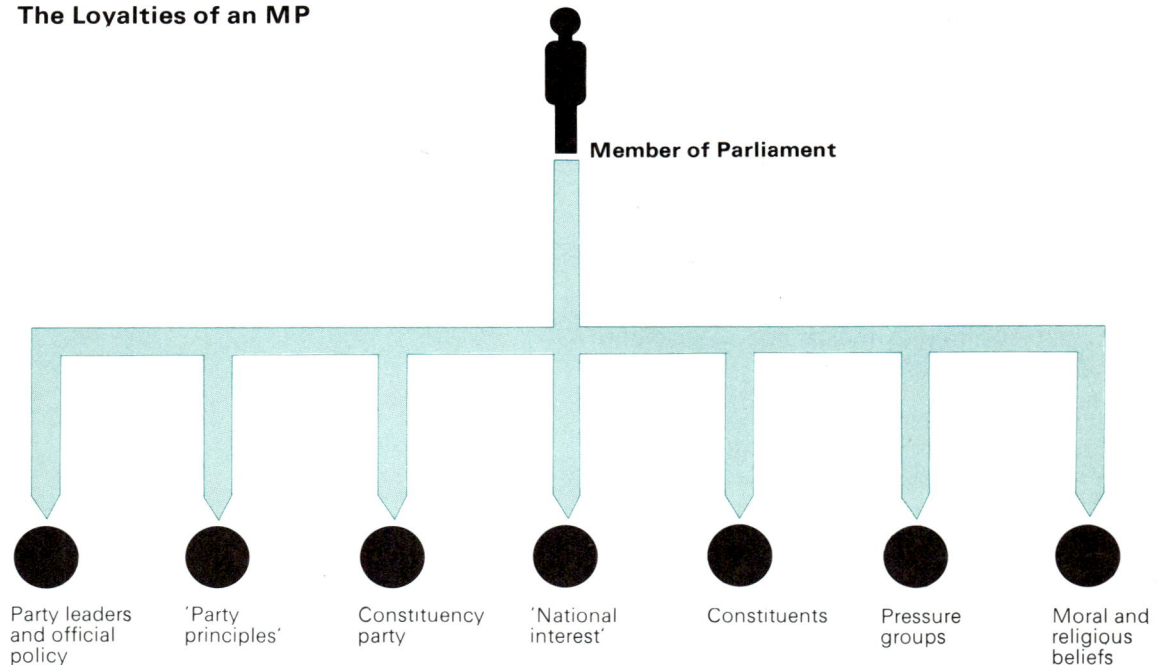

Member of Parliament

| Party leaders and official policy | 'Party principles' | Constituency party | 'National interest' | Constituents | Pressure groups | Moral and religious beliefs |

go on as national leader. Within days, Winston Churchill took over.

Perhaps the most difficult of all conflicts facing MPs are clashes between their normal political loyalties and their religious or moral beliefs. Party leaders try to minimise such conflicts by allowing *free votes* in the Commons when obvious 'matters of conscience' are debated. It would be senseless and wrong to turn these into party issues.

How important are back-benchers?

Ordinary rank-and-file MPs rarely criticise their leaders in public, and their support can nearly always be relied upon in important Commons votes. Consequently it is often assumed that back-benchers are some kind of 'lobby fodder' who do as they are told and hardly ever answer back. Perhaps this is true of some; but most MPs are quick to show their dissatisfaction with party policy 'behind the scenes'—through informal contacts, private meetings, letters and so on. The fact that open clashes between party leaders and their back-

Sometimes an MP's basic loyalty to official party leaders and policies will conflict with other loyalties. In most cases such conflicts are temporary, but every now and again an MP will break with his party—and perhaps with politics altogether.

benchers are rare does not necessarily mean that back-benchers are 'yes men'. It is more likely to be an indication of the success of party leaders in assessing the feelings of their supporters.

Back-bench MPs have only a slight chance of speaking in important debates. But at Question Time and in Adjournment Debates and committees they do have opportunities for making their presence felt. And outside Parliament, in their constituencies, they keep closely in touch with the electorate. The fact that ordinary members of the public 'lobby' MPs in Parliament, in order to make their grievances heard, shows the importance people attach to 'having the ear' of an MP. Back-bench MPs are a vital link in the chain of communication between party leaders and the electorate at large.

To write, discuss and find out

1 If you were an MP, what Private Members' Bill would you want to introduce? Try drafting out the main points, and then write a short version of the speech you would make in presenting the Bill at its Second Reading.

2 Which areas of government expenditure would you like to see

a reduced;

b increased?

3a Why is Question Time in the Commons important?

b Look at the questions that were asked in our extract from a typical week in July 1971. What do you think were the most likely reasons these MPs had for asking them—to press for action on an issue, to obtain information, or to embarrass the government?

4 Imagine you are an MP for a mining constituency and your party, at present in government, has decided to close pits in your area. What factors would you take into account in deciding where your main loyalties should lie?

5 What sorts of things might an ambitious MP do in order to further his political career?

6 Try to *find out* where, and how often, your MP holds 'surgeries'. Study the local papers and make a note of any publicity given to your MP in connection with constituency matters.

7 Using the press, radio and TV, try to follow,

a a Commons debate on a major issue;

b the passage of a Bill through Parliament.

What kind of publicity is given in the mass media? Are there any signs of disagreement *within* the parties?

The House of Lords

8

Seven hundred years ago, when humble knights from the counties and citizens from the towns were first invited to Parliament, 'the Commons', as they were called, had little political influence. The King's most important advisers in Parliament were his barons and bishops, known as 'the Lords'. These great landowners were the richest and most powerful people in the kingdom, and no monarch could afford to ignore their views.

The Lords remained the most influential part of Parliament for several hundred years after they were joined by the Commons in the thirteenth century. But gradually 'commoners' began to gain wealth and influence through trade, banking and manufacturing; and the power of their House of Parliament grew at the expense of the Lords. In the eighteenth and

The composition of the House of Lords

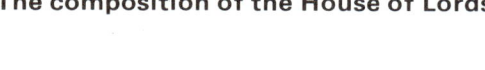

Conservative 351
Labour 116
Liberal 41

In addition there are about 100 **'Independents'.** Bishops and Law Lords are excluded—they are supposed to be above party politics. The remainder of peers have either not stated a preference or (as in the case of 300 hereditary peers) never turned up.

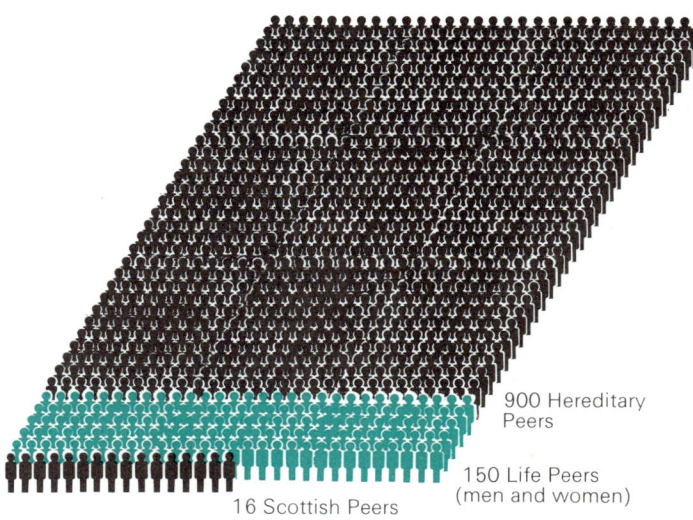

900 Hereditary Peers

150 Life Peers (men and women)

16 Scottish Peers

Peers

Bishops

2 Archbishops

24 Bishops

Law Lords 9

nineteenth centuries *both* Houses were powerful, and prime ministers could be chosen from either. However the Lords was still dominated by rich landowners, as it had been in the Middle Ages. Apart from the bishops of the Church of England, members of the Lords were not elected. The right to belong to the House was *hereditary* (handed on from father to son, along with family titles, property and other possessions).

Decline of the Lords

The importance of the Lords was understandable in the days when few people had the right to vote for MPs, and when *both* Houses of Parliament represented the more privileged groups in society. But as we have seen, in the nineteenth and early twentieth centuries the right to vote was gradually extended to include all men and women. It became generally accepted that the people as a whole should *elect* their political leaders. Consequently the power of the (non-elected) Lords became difficult to justify.

Many people thought it wrong that the Lords should be allowed to reject Bills that had been passed by the elected House of Commons. Two famous occasions when this happened were in 1886, when the Liberal Government attempted to give Home Rule to Ireland, and in 1909, when another Liberal Government had its Budget (Finance Bill) thrown out by the Lords. On the second occasion, the government had proposed

The House of Lords. The object in the centre, like a sofa without arms, is the Woolsack—the seat of the Lord Chancellor, chairman of the House (and a member of the Cabinet).

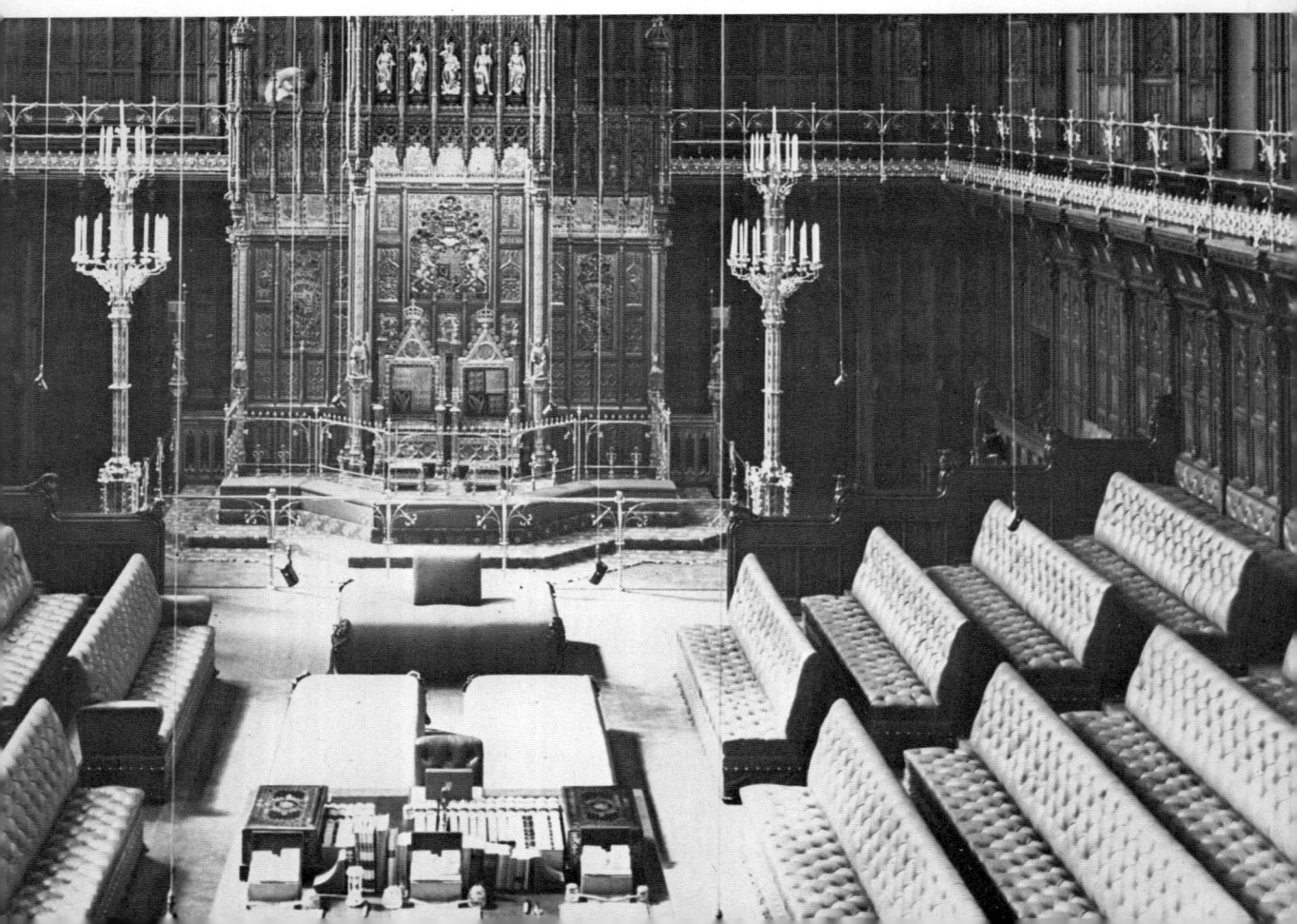

to increase taxation on the rich (including the introduction of land taxes) and use some of the money to pay for social welfare schemes. This raised a storm of protest among the wealthy landowners in the Lords. The Upper House rejected the Budget, even though it had become a *convention* that Bills connected with government finance should not be interfered with in this way.

The time had come for a showdown between the two Houses of Parliament. After a bitter struggle the Commons got its way and forced through a Parliament Act (1911) which drastically cut the powers of the Upper House. The Lords were no longer allowed to prevent the passage of 'Money Bills', and they could not hold up other sorts of Bills for more than two years. The 1911 Act only got through the Lords after the prime minister and the King had threatened to create over 300 new peers who would vote with the Liberal Government. The 'delaying power' of the Lords (its right to hold up Bills) was further reduced, from two years to one, in a second Parliament Act passed by a Labour Government in 1949.

During this century the only times when the Lords have rejected (or tried to reject) government Bills have been during periods of Liberal or Labour control of the Commons. This is perhaps not surprising, since the Conservative Party always has a comfortable majority in the Upper House. It was the domination of the Lords by one party which made the Parliament Acts essential. For if the Upper House had kept its traditional powers it would have given the Conservatives a permanent advantage in the British political system.

Why do we still have an Upper House?

It might seem that the House of Lords, deprived of most of its original powers, could just as well be abolished altogether. But it does in fact do useful work as the 'Second Chamber' of Parliament. All Bills have to pass through the Lords, and in the process legal 'loopholes' and

Lord Hailsham (above) gave up his peerage in 1963 and entered the Commons, as plain Quintin Hogg. But in 1970 he resumed his title in order to become Lord Chancellor.

other difficulties that the Commons may have overlooked can be brought to light. Where this happens, the Lords usually suggest *amendments* (changes) in the Bill, and these are often accepted by the Commons.

Virtually all *Private* Bills (which generally give powers to local authorities) are introduced into the Lords first, where special committees examine them in detail. When this work is finished, such Bills normally pass quickly through the Commons. *Public* Bills which have no clear division on party lines sometimes start off in the Lords too—especially if they deal with the sorts of moral issues that go to a free vote in the Commons. The Lower House is much the busier of the two, so it is a great help to have the bulk of the work on some Bills done by the Lords.

From time to time the House of Lords holds full-scale debates on matters of public interest which the Commons may not have been able to discuss at length. Examples include the preservation of areas of natural beauty, the rights of women in employment, and the treatment of young offenders. In debates of this kind the Lords can call on a lot of expert opinion. The life peers for instance, who are chosen because of their high standing in some aspect of public life, can speak with authority on matters close to their experience. Big debates in the Lords are well reported in the press and on radio and television. In this way they make a valuable contribution to political discussion.

The State Opening of Parliament, in 1970. Members of both Houses assemble in the Lords to hear the Queen's Speech: a statement of government policy for the coming year, written by the prime minister.

House of Lords reform

Since the reduction of the Lords' 'delaying power' to one year (1949) there have been a number of important changes in the membership and day-to-day running of the House. Life peerages, available to both men and women, were first awarded in 1958; and these have since become the usual method of recruitment to the Lords. (In fact no new hereditary peerages have been given since 1964.) Nowadays an 'attendance fee' is paid to cover the expenses of those attending the House, in the hope of encouraging more members to take part regularly. And since 1963 it has been possible for members of the Lords to *renounce* (give up) their titles and seats in the Upper House. Before that date several leading MPs who were sons of hereditary peers had been forced to leave the Commons, much against their will, when their fathers died and passed on their titles.

Many people feel that these changes have not gone far enough, and that the Lords should be completely reformed. An overwhelming majority of its members are still hereditary peers, who owe their place in Parliament to an accident of birth. And the permanent Conservative majority in the Lords means that during the last year of office of a Labour government the Upper House can, if it so wishes, block the passage of a Bill. This happened in 1949, when the Lords prevented a Labour government from nationalising the steel industry. A general election was due the following year, and the government had to fight—and win—the election before it could get the Bill through.

Should the 'delaying powers' be abolished altogether? Here are two opposing views:

There could arise a matter of great constitutional importance, on which there was known to be a deep division of opinion in the country. . . . In a case of this kind, it seems to me that the House of Lords has a right, and perhaps a duty, to use its powers, not to make a decision, but to afford the people of this country and members of the House of Commons a period for reflection and time for views to be expressed. (Lord Carrington)

We claim that it is for the elected representatives of the people to decide whether an issue is or is not to be the subject of Parliamentary activity. . . .
We do not accept . . . that this House, entirely unrepresentative, shall be the final arbiter [judge] as to what is and what is not the opinion of the people. (Viscount Addison)

Whether or not it should be allowed to delay legislation, most politicians agree that *some kind* of Second Chamber is essential—to save the Commons time, and to inspire second thoughts on some of the government measures that come before it. But there are wide differences of opinion as to the sort of chamber it should be. There is probably general agreement that it would be unfair for one party to have a permanent majority, as at present. And most politicians would accept a reduction in the powers of hereditary peers, if not a complete end to their political influence.

A far-reaching reform of the Upper House was in fact put forward in 1968, during Harold Wilson's Labour ministry. It was proposed that the hereditary peers should become non-voting members for the rest of their lives, and that their descendants should *not* have the right to sit in the House. The government party was to be given a majority of voting peers over the other parties (though not a majority in the Lords as a whole, because many life peers are not attached to parties). It was also proposed that the delaying power of the Lords should come down to six months.

There was general support for these reforms among the leaders of the major parties in the Commons. But they were defeated by an unusual alliance between reformist Labour MPs (for whom the proposals did not go far enough) and traditionalist Conservatives (for whom they went *too* far)! But this is unlikely to be the end of the story. The question of Lords' reform will no doubt be revived before long.

To write, discuss and find out

1 Do you think there can ever be any justification for a non-elected Chamber being able to delay legislation?

2 What advantages are there for the *Commons* in having a Second Chamber?

3 Make a list of *ten* people you would like to see given life peerages. Give reasons for your choices.

4 'If the Upper House is weak there is no point in having it; if it is strong it is objectionable.'

Explain what the writer means, and say whether or not you agree. Give reasons for your views.

5 In what ways would *you* reform the House of Lords?

6 *Find out* about activities in the Lords during one full week, and keep a diary. What publicity did the Lords get in the mass media?

From what has been said in the last six chapters, it should be clear that Parliament occupies a central position in British politics. But *how far* does its influence go—especially in relation to the government, the Civil Service and the mass media? In this chapter we shall retrace some of our steps and try to assess just how important Parliament really is.

The place of Parliament in British politics

First of all, Parliament is the *legislature* (the place where laws are passed). As well as making new laws, it can change or abolish any of the existing ones if it wishes. Consequently the decisions of one Parliament cannot bind future Parliaments—no law can be passed which could not be changed at some future date. During

A newly formed French Cabinet, 1953. Unlike the UK Parliament, which normally maintains the elected government in power, the French National Assembly at this time made and unmade a succession of short-lived governments.

ELECTION FORUM
ELECTION FORUM

The Conservative Leader answers BBC viewers' questions during the 1970 election campaign.

World War Two for instance, Parliament even decided not to hold a general election. One was due by law in 1940, but because of the threat to national security the Parliament of the time prolonged its own life until 1945.

In practice the legislative powers of Parliament are in the hands of the prime minister and his Cabinet, so long as they can keep a party majority in the Commons. However this majority in turn depends on the result of a general election. So the *authority* of a government (its *right* to rule) is based on the people's overall preference for that party and its leaders. The government can claim that it has been chosen by the people in a fair and open contest for power.

It follows that the second important job of Parliament is to *maintain a government*. It does not pick a government (that is done by the electorate). It simply ensures that the government chosen by the people is able to rule effectively—which is in fact achieved through party organisation in the Commons.

Although the government is normally able to 'control' Parliament, this does not mean that it can do just as it pleases. Parliament examines and *criticises* the actions of government—a third important aspect of its work. There are some parliaments or political assemblies in the world which are little more than 'rubber stamps' for official policy, because all (or practically all) their members are devoted

supporters of the government. But in Britain the existence of an official opposition in Parliament ensures regular public criticism. Government MPs too will often express disagreement, at least privately, if they feel that their party's leaders are following the wrong policies.

Parliament's ability to act as a public 'watchdog' on government depends to a large extent on *ministerial responsibility* (see Chapter 5). Ministers are expected to account for the work of their departments and take responsibility for complaints against civil servants. This is important where the rights of ordinary individuals are concerned. MPs can question ministers on behalf of constituents who are dissatisfied with the actions of government departments. But in the end this depends on ministers being willing to *accept* responsibility. In one or two recent cases ministers have been reluctant to do so.

These three main aspects of Parliament's work help to make it the most important *forum* (public centre of discussion) in British politics. Parliament is the arena where the political parties fight their major battles. And consequently it is important in the political education of the people. Debates, questions and the passage of Bills all add to public awareness of what is going on in government—through reports in the press and on radio and television.

Many of the political issues which are given prominence in the mass media have their beginnings in the day-to-day activities of

Parliament. For instance in 1973 an attempt was made to re-introduce capital punishment through a Private Member's Bill. The mass media were quick to respond. A flood of articles, editorials and letters in the press, and discussion programmes on radio and television, kept the main issues in front of the public for several weeks. Once the Bill had been debated in the Commons, and rejected, the excitement quickly subsided.

Shortcomings of the parliamentary system

Let us now take a more critical look at the work of Parliament. For it is clear that not all its tasks are carried out as efficiently as they could be.

Checks on government

How effective is Parliament in examining legislation and in criticising government policy? Are MPs expert enough to carry out these tasks properly? Certainly many members have detailed knowledge of particular areas of government, but this is not always put to its best use. For instance when a Bill is examined in detail 'upstairs', it is not sent to a committee of MPs who have special knowledge of the subject. It goes to one of six committees merely labelled A to F.

It is true that there are *some* Commons committees which specialise in particular aspects of government. In Chapter 7 we referred to two special committees which keep an eye on government spending. And another example is the Select Committee on Nationalised Industries, which reports on the activities of state run businesses. But there is no system of expert committees in important areas such as foreign affairs, education, health services and so on. If such committees did exist, and were allowed to investigate policies in detail, MPs would be able to criticise the government more effectively. However this would not be popular with ministers, who might feel that their control over policy decisions was being weakened.

At present MPs are severely handicapped in their attempts to investigate the work of government. Very few can afford to employ their own research staff; and the Commons library, with only twelve researchers, has over 2000 requests for information every year. On the other hand, ministers have an army of civil servants to give them information and help them prepare speeches and answers to questions in Parliament. Senior civil servants often spend hours briefing a minister before Question Time. Yet in their dealings with ordinary MPs, civil servants tend not to give information unless it is asked for. This means that MPs need to know in advance the right questions to ask.

The rights of individuals

How effective are MPs in defending the rights of their constituents? Obviously there is a great deal of variation here, because some members are more energetic and conscientious than others. Most, if not all, MPs hold some kind of 'surgery' in their constituencies. But it is not really enough for an MP just to make himself available, because many people who need his help will not come of their own accord. There is a need for MPs to actively seek out cases that need investigating. But it is hardly surprising that they are reluctant to do this, since many are already overworked. Even at ordinary surgeries MPs lack support. It would be very useful, for example, if at every surgery a solicitor and a local councillor were available.

Constituency matters are often raised at Question Time in the Commons. But even here MPs' efforts are not always successful. If they get an unhelpful answer from a minister, for example, it is difficult for them to challenge it. This was the main reason for the appointment, in 1967, of the Parliamentary Commissioner, or *Ombudsman*. Assisted by a staff of about sixty, his task is to investigate complaints against government departments. He can only deal with cases sent to him by MPs (he cannot be approached directly by ordinary members of the public). And complaints against the police, nationalised industries and local authorities are not included in his work.

The *Ombudsman* and his staff try to find out whether departments have kept to their own rules and made decisions in the proper way. Unfortunately on some occasions injustice to individuals can result even when the rules *are* properly applied. Nevertheless the *Ombudsman* is in a stronger position than an MP, because he can question civil servants directly and ask to see documents relating to the case. He does not have to be satisfied just with the answers given by ministers.

Sir Edmund Compton, Britain's first Parliamentary Commissioner or Ombudsman, *pictured in 1966 just before his appointment.*

Parliament and the people

In recent years Parliament seems to have lost some of its importance as a link between the government and the public. Some groups which seek to influence the government (known as 'pressure groups', see Chapter 11) often bypass MPs and try to make direct contact with ministers and top-ranking officials. The most effective place to exert pressure is at the very centre of power—the government itself.

Parliament can also be bypassed by the press, radio and television. It is true that most political issues that are given publicity in the

'The most effective place to exert pressure is at the very centre of power'. Here we see a delegation of Clyde shipyard workers outside 10 Downing Street in June 1971. They came from Glasgow to put to the Prime Minister their case for keeping open Upper Clyde Ship-builders, which was threatened with closure.

Television cameras at work in the West German Bundestag *(parliament).*

mass media stem from Parliament. But the media sometimes play a more positive part in politics. Ministers may arrange to appear on television in order to explain policies to the public directly, instead of through reports of parliamentary debates. And some of the most searching enquiries into government actions are made by newspapers or by probing interviewers on television. Nowadays a poor performance on television can be much more damaging to a politician's career than a poor showing in the Commons.

So public discussion and criticism of the government is shared by Parliament and the mass media. And the importance of the media has increased in modern society. This is understandable, since newspapers and broadcasting

organisations (unlike MPs) have the money and staff to carry out detailed investigations. However the mass media have not 'taken over' Parliament's task. Rather they act as *additional* watchdogs on government. As the affairs of government get more and more complicated, it is useful to have as many watchdogs as possible.

Only a tiny number of people actually visit Parliament and observe debates from the public gallery. And yet, unlike many other countries, Britain has no 'live' radio or television coverage of parliamentary proceedings. The opponents of live reporting in the Commons argue that it would destroy the atmosphere of the House.

They say that speakers would be more concerned with their impact on the listening or viewing public than on the members present in the Chamber. And the sight of the frequently half empty benches (while MPs are working on committees or in their constituencies) might be misunderstood.

Against these arguments it could be said that if Parliament really is the national *forum* for politics then it should move with the times and use the newer forms of communication. Televised debates on a major issue such as British entry into the EEC could have done much to increase public interest and understanding. Many people feel that parliamentary traditions are less important than the need to involve the public more directly in politics.

To write, discuss and find out

1 How is it possible for Parliament to be a major political *forum* when only a handful of people actually watch its debates from the public gallery?

2 What are the factors which make it difficult for MPs to do their work efficiently in

a the House of Commons;

b their constituencies?

3 What are the main 'watchdogs' on a government's use of power? Which do you think are the most effective?

4a Do you think parliamentary debates should be televised? Give reasons for your views. views.

b Assuming that the televising of Parliament were to be accepted by a majority of MPs, what form would you like to see the programmes take? Should debates be transmitted 'live', as they happen, or should they be put into the form of 'edited highlights' at peak viewing hours? What are the difficulties involved in each of these alternatives?

5 *Find out* how daily proceedings in Parliament are reported on BBC radio, and listen to one or two of the programmes. Do you think these broadcasts are helpful in informing the public of what is going on? How do you think they might be improved?

6 *Find out* more about the work of the Parliamentary Commissioner for Administration (the *Ombudsman*). His office is at Church House, Great Smith Street, London, SW1.

The Monarchy

The British monarchy is a perfect example of the way in which political institutions can be transformed while remaining outwardly the same. For many hundreds of years the 'government' of Britain was the monarch. He (or she) was the centre of power and authority, which passed on through inheritance. Some monarchs, and their subjects, believed that the right to rule was God-given. However this idea went out of favour in the seventeenth century.

Today we still have the monarchy, and, strictly according to the law, the Queen has far-reaching powers. She has the right to reject Bills passed by Parliament, to declare war, to pardon criminals and so forth. But in practice these powers are exercised on her behalf by the elected government. The constitutional convention is quite clear: that the monarch acts only on the advice of the prime minister and government.

Two contrasting examples of the duties of a British monarch.
Below Queen Elizabeth II meets her Prime Minister (then Harold Wilson) for a routine discussion of affairs of state.
Right King George VI inspects bomb damage in London during World War Two.

Why has the monarchy survived?

It was once said that, in time, Europe would have only five kings: hearts, clubs, diamonds, spades and England. Certainly since 1900 the number of 'crowned heads of Europe' has fallen dramatically. And the few that remain have virtually no political power. Yet in the United Kingdom the monarchy has, if anything, increased in popularity as its power has declined. This loss of power is in fact one of the reasons for its survival. The monarchy is separated from party politics and the day-to-day business of government. Consequently its popularity is unaffected by the failures, or successes, of governments.

The *political impartiality* of the monarch is seen at the official State Opening of Parliament —the one day in the year when the Queen actually sits in Parliament. Members of both Houses assemble in the Lords to hear the 'speech from the throne'. This does not contain the Queen's personal views; it is a statement of government policy for the coming session, written by the prime minister.

Although the monarch has no political power, she still has the arduous task of being the *non-political* head of state. A vast range of duties, from foreign tours to officially opening public buildings or unveiling statues, keeps the royal family extremely busy. The monarch and members of her family take an interest in many aspects of national life. They are as much concerned with religion, the arts, sport, industry and commerce, as with politics.

The majority of the people seem to enjoy the glamour, pomp and pageantry of royal occasions. Colourful parades and ceremonies have a place in every society. They help to strengthen the bonds between people, and when they are connected with politics they gave a certain dignity to the affairs of government. The monarchy is a symbol of many of Britain's proudest traditions. Whatever evidence we have of public attitudes towards the monarchy suggests that there is little demand for its abolition.

The non-political head of state

All countries have some kind of official head of state. As we know, republics (countries without a monarchy) have presidents. There are two main sorts of presidents. Some are highly political and elected into office by the people (as in the USA and France). Others are mere ceremonial figures (as in Italy and West Germany).

The first kind of president has the problems of separating government responsibilities from non-political affairs of state. The political nature of his office may well make him less convincing when he has to act as a symbol of national unity. The second kind of president concentrates on the social and ceremonial side of government and leaves the prime minister to get on with matters of political importance. In Britain, the ancient traditions of the royal family and the respect most people have for it, makes the monarch ideally suited to the role of non-political head of state.

An important part of the work of any head of state is visiting other countries and, in return, entertaining foreign presidents or monarchs. The British royal family gives to such occasions a sense of awe and majesty that no presidency could hope to achieve. However some people argue that there are disadvantages, and even dangers, in having a monarchy. Let us consider two of the most common objections.

First, it is pointed out that although the monarchy has lost political *power* it still plays an important part in the official business of government. Only the Queen may dissolve Parliament; her signature is necessary before any Bill can become law, she has to approve the appointment of ministers, and so forth. All this can lead people into misunderstanding how the British political system works. For instance it was believed by some opponents of British entry into the EEC (1973) that the Queen could have prevented it from happening if she had refused to sign the necessary Bills.

Second, opponents of the monarchy often argue that the idea of the royal family as 'special' people, at the top of some kind of social pyramid, encourages snobbery. Nowadays, of course, the royal family represents the whole nation—not just wealthy and privileged members of society. Nevertheless, through their education, tastes and pursuits and their own wealth they are bound to be cut off to some extent from ordinary men and women.

Whether or not these criticisms are justified is largely a matter of opinion. But one thing there can be no doubt about: the monarchy has the respect and loyalty of the majority of British people. Its position in the constitution reflects two vitally important (although contradictory) features of British politics—continuity with the past, yet the ability to change when circumstances demand it.

To write, discuss and find out

1 'The Queen reigns but does not rule.'
In what ways does this sum up the position of the monarchy in the British constitution?
2 Do you think royal pageantry serves any useful purpose?
3 How can a monarch make it easier for a prime minister to do the job for which he was elected?
4 Organise a debate on the motion: The monarchy should be abolished and most of its wealth given to the nation.
5 *Find out* which European countries still have a monarchy, and what the main similarities and differences are between continental monarchs and Queen Elizabeth II.

Visiting other countries is an important part of a monarch's duties. Here the Queen and Prince Philip are pictured during a royal tour of Sierra Leone, 1961.

Political communication: parties, pressure groups, mass media   11

The lifeblood of the British political system is the continual exchange of ideas, information and arguments between politicians and the public. In this chapter we shall look more closely at the ways in which such *political communication* takes place. Obviously the political parties play a central part. But there are many other groups and organisations which represent powerful interests and opinions. Some of these, such as trade unions, employers' associations, various sorts of 'protest groups' and even sections of the mass media, will regularly try to influence government decisions. Other groups with narrower interests, including motoring associations, sports clubs and the like, will only rarely become involved in national or local government

Political parties

Practically all countries have political parties, although some have only one party while others have a large number. In Britain the parties act as *two-way* channels of communication between political leaders and the people. But in some other states the communication is nearly all one way—downwards from the leaders. Where this happens (as in a number of Communist states) a party's main task may be to reinforce the government's control over the people.

In Britain there are the two main parties; a third (the Liberals) with a large following in the country, if not in the Commons, and a range of much smaller ones. However the major political battle is between Conservative and Labour. It may seem strange that all the different interests and opinions of the British people are reduced to such a limited choice. Why is this? If we have a large variety of political views why is there not a similar variety of political parties? The answer really lies in the search for *power*.

Parties and power

Political parties exist in order to become the government. In Britain this means that they must gain a majority of seats in the House of Commons. To obtain such a majority, with 630 seats at stake, calls for nationwide party organisation. It also calls for compromise—a willingness on the part of those who seek power to work with people of similar, even if not identical, views.

If all the differing shades of opinion in Britain were reflected in separate political parties, it would be virtually impossible for any one party to win a majority in the Commons. Governments would have to be formed by an alliance or *coalition* of several parties who agreed to act together. This happens in countries (like Italy) which have a large number of parties. But in Britain the two main parties are *already* coalitions. They bind together a number of smaller groups which have some (but not all) aims in common and are therefore able to reach compromises over policy.

The tendency for there to be just two main parties in Britain is largely due to the electoral system. As we saw in Chapter 3, only one candidate is elected in each constituency, and the votes cast for unsuccessful candidates do not count at all. Consequently small parties find it very difficult to win seats, even though they may have quite a large following spread thinly across the country. This is the problem facing the Liberals. Many people feel that they would be 'wasting' their vote if they did not use it to support one of the major parties.

Conservative and Labour
What do the two main parties stand for? This is a difficult question, partly because policies change with circumstances and partly because the parties are coalitions, reflecting many different shades of opinion. There are bound to

Hitler addresses a Youth Rally at Nuremberg, 1938. In Nazi Germany, political communication was all one way—downwards from the party leaders to the people.

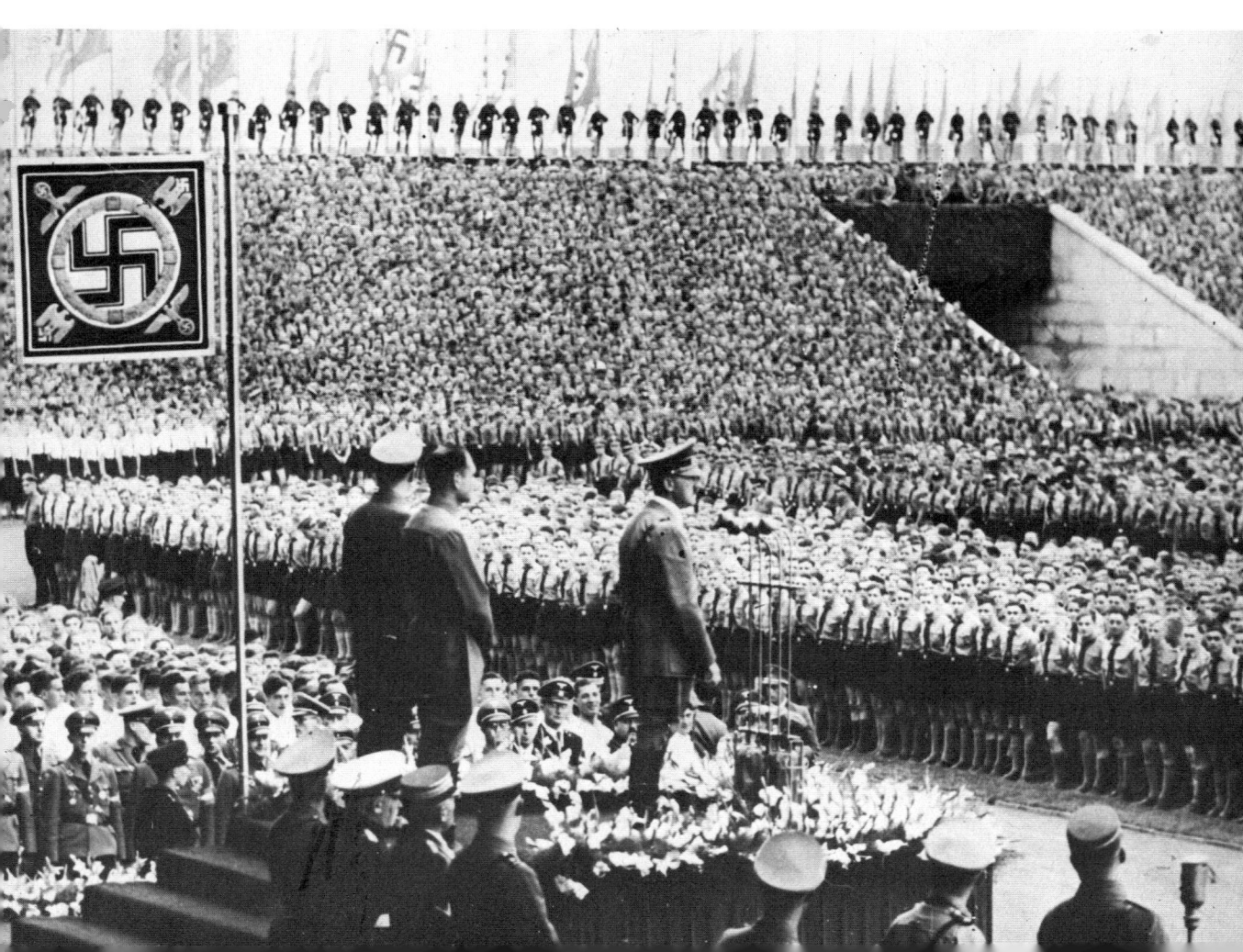

Groupings within the Labour and Conservative Parties

Together such groups largely decide the form that each party will take

Monday Club, Bow Group, **Fabian Society** and other political clubs or societies (some of which carry out their own research)

MPs (Some with large personal following)

Constituency parties

Party Leaders

Full Time Officials **(Central Office, Transport House)**

'Pressure Groups' Some are closely involved with a particular party; e.g. **Nuclear Disarmament and Labour.** Others appeal to all parties, but are more likely to get a sympathetic hearing on one side or the other; e.g. **Anti-Apartheid Movement (Labour), Farmers' and Shopkeepers' Associations (Conservative)**

Young Conservatives Young Socialists

Ministers (when in power)

Local Government Councillors

Business and Financial Interests. Trade Unions, Cooperative Party (both sponsor Labour MPs)

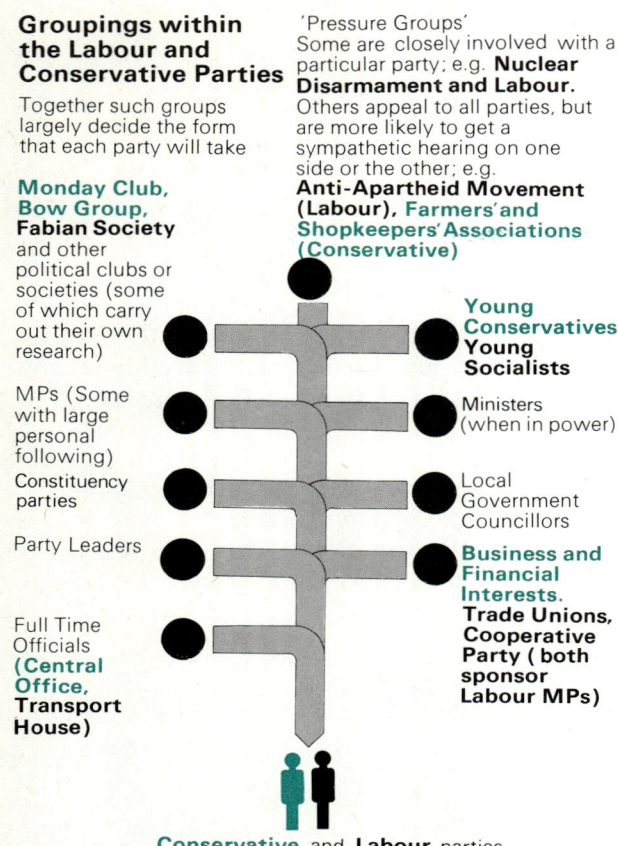

Conservative and **Labour** parties

A party membership card. Only a tiny proportion of those who vote for political parties in elections actually 'belong' to them.

be occasions when groups within the party disagree. Nevertheless all members of a party will have certain basic beliefs or principles, which add up to a kind of 'party image'.

We saw in Chapter 2 that the Labour Party arose out of the trade union movement, with the main aim of increasing the representation of the working classes in Parliament. So over the years it has worked to safeguard the rights of trade unions to organise and strike. In more general terms Labour supporters like to think of themselves as champions of the 'underdogs' of society. Consequently they are the staunchest supporters of the 'Welfare State'.

We should be careful about this, however, because the Conservative Party fully accepts the need for social services. The main difference between the parties is to do with the *sorts* of services that should be provided. The Con-

servatives prefer to be *selective*—to concentrate on helping those most in need, such as the very lowest paid workers and their families. The Labour Party, on the other hand, argues that most social services should be freely available to everyone—as used to happen, for example, when free milk was given to *all* children of school age.*

However it is in the management of the country's economy that some of the most important party differences are to be found. The Conservatives generally prefer to see industry privately owned, whereas the Labour Party favours a good deal of *nationalisation*— the compulsory transfer of private industries into public ownership. The Conservative view

---

*For some of the arguments behind these views, see *The Social Services* (Series 2)

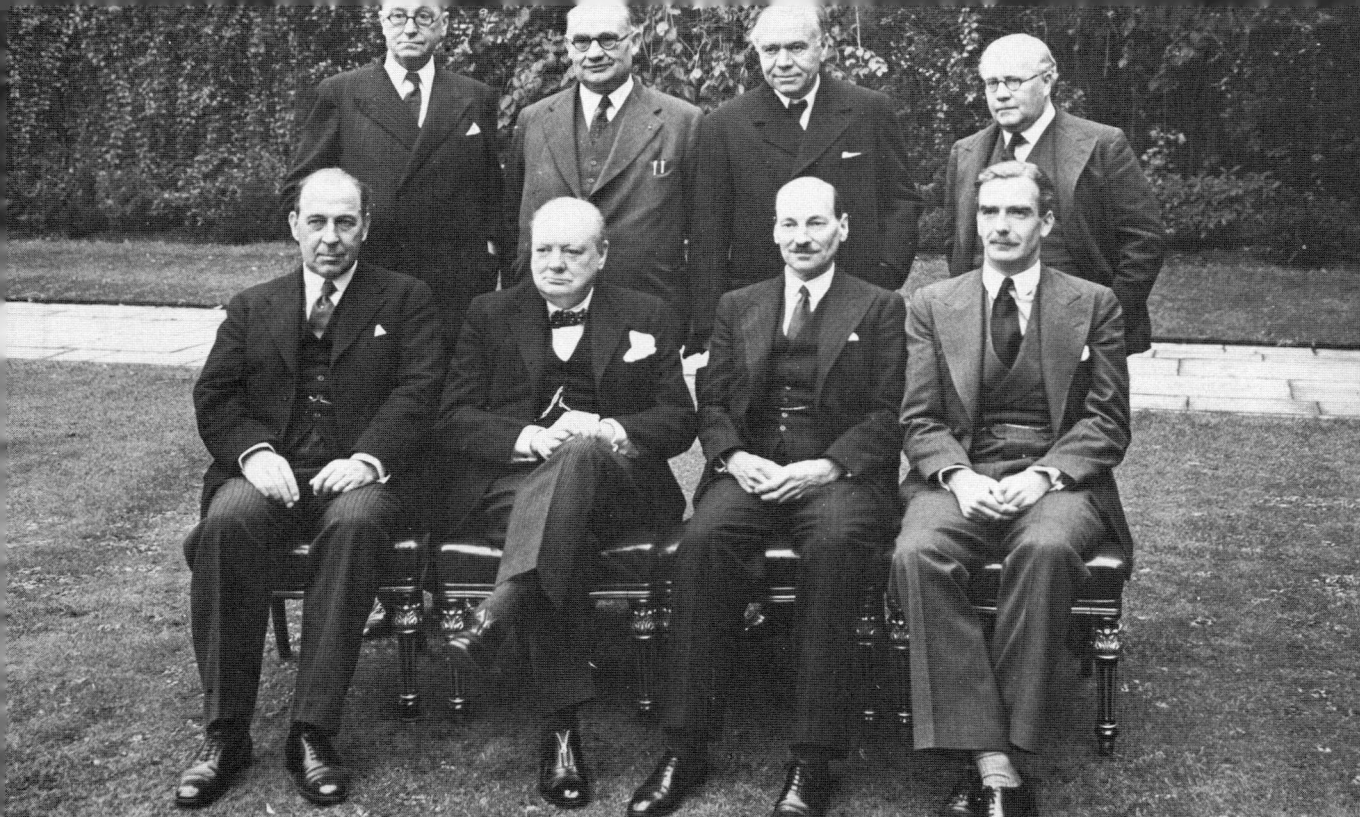

is that competition between a number of private firms is the surest road to prosperity and a fair deal for the customer. But Labour supporters argue that state controlled industries allow for more long-term planning of the national economy, and are more likely to be run for the benefit of the community as a whole.

The Conservative belief in 'private enterprise' is linked to the Party's policies on taxation. Conservatives believe that go-ahead individuals should not be discouraged from making extra effort by very high rates of taxation on top incomes. They accept that the richest should pay proportionately more in taxes, but do not want this to go too far. The Labour Party has less sympathy with the problems of the high tax-payer. When taxes have to be increased the usual Labour view is that much of the extra money should come from the wealthiest members of society.

There are other important differences between the parties that we cannot go into here. Education policy is one example—especially the future of public schools, which the Conservatives

During great emergencies of the past, leaders of the main parties have joined together in a coalition *government. Here we see Winston Churchill's wartime Coalition Cabinet (1940).*

support and large sections of the Labour Party would like to abolish. But in the end perhaps the best way of understanding party differences is to look closely at their *supporters* and the social backgrounds they come from. This is done in Chapter 12, when we come to consider voting behaviour.

Is party conflict taken too far?

The two major parties try to unite many different shades of opinion and offer the electorate a clear choice—Conservative or Labour. This is not without its disadvantages. Quite small differences between the parties can be magnified out of all proportion. And complicated issues are often over-simplified, or reduced to petty slogans—'Let's Go With Labour', or 'Life is Better Under the Conservatives'.

Some party conflict is very trivial—as for instance when politicians refuse to give credit where it is due, implying that anything done by the other side *must* be wrong! Occasionally it has harmful effects, as when rival politicians give misleading accounts of each others' policies or try to outdo each other in making lavish promises to the electorate.

Some people think that these aspects of party politics are so distasteful that it would be better to have a Coalition Government. In other words the 'best men' in each party should join together to form a government that would be free from party squabbles. This is possible in times of great national emergency such as a war, when the whole country unites against a common enemy. But in normal circumstances it would be very difficult to get the necessary agreement between the major parties. In most cases 'party squabbles' do arise out of genuine differences of opinion.

The great value of having two or more parties is that the government is open to sustained criticism. And *alternative* policies are continually being put forward. This is the productive side of party conflict. Furthermore the parties help to stimulate public interest in politics. They encourage political discussion and argument; they provide candidates and urge people to vote at election time. All in all, the parties are vital

One of the most famous pressure groups in British history was the highly successful Anti-Corn Law League of the 1840s, which worked for the abolition of taxes on food imports. Here we see a leading spokesman, Richard Cobden, MP, addressing fellow members of the League's ruling Council in 1846—the year in which the Corn Laws were repealed by Parliament.

channels of communication amongst and between politicians and the public.

Pressure groups

Unlike parties, pressure groups do not seek political power themselves. They aim to influence those who have it. And whereas parties have to work out policies to cover the whole range of government activity, the interests of pressure groups are more limited in scope. Often they have just one basic aim, such as nuclear disarmament, comprehensive education, or the banning of 'obscene' language on radio and television.

Growth and types of pressure groups

Pressure groups have a long history. One of the most famous of the last century was the Anti-Corn Law League, which in the 1840s ran a nationwide campaign to abolish taxes on food imports. Millions of copies of pamphlets and

Types of pressure groups

Permanent

a Groups formed *to protect particular interests*, e.g. trade unions, CBI (Confederation of British Industry), National Farmers' Union, AA (Automobile Association) and RAC (Royal Automobile Club), Society of Motor Manufacturers

b Groups whose members are *united by a 'cause' or set of beliefs* (rather than by a defence of their personal position, as in **a**) e.g. National Council for Civil Liberties, CND (Campaign for Nuclear Disarmament), Anti-Apartheid Movement, Viewers' and Listeners' Association

Temporary or 'One Issue' Groups. Likely to be disbanded when their case is won or lost.

a Concerned with *national* issues, e.g. parents of thalidomide children; for and against entry into EEC; for and against retaining grammar schools

b Concerned with *local or regional* issues, e.g. groups in favour of certain local amenities such as street crossings and public lavatories; groups opposed to the building of particular motorways, airports, etc.

Methods used by national pressure groups

1
Representatives on 'official' committees; contact with civil servants and ministers – through meetings, letters, phone calls, lunches, and even activities such as playing golf

Used by groups accepted as important and useful by the government

2
Delegations to see ministers or 'lobby' MPs in Parliament; attempts to gain the support of particular MPs

Used by groups which have little direct contact with government (and also by 'important' groups if they are not successful with **1**)

3
Public campaigns – including press advertising, demonstrations, marches, sit-ins, strikes, etc.

Used by groups which would otherwise have difficulty in attracting the attention of the government (and also by more powerful groups, to reinforce **1** and **2**)

N.B. *The most effective pressure groups are not necessarily the noisiest*

**Pressure Groups involved in a typical
'One Issue' local controversy:**
Re-organisation of secondary education

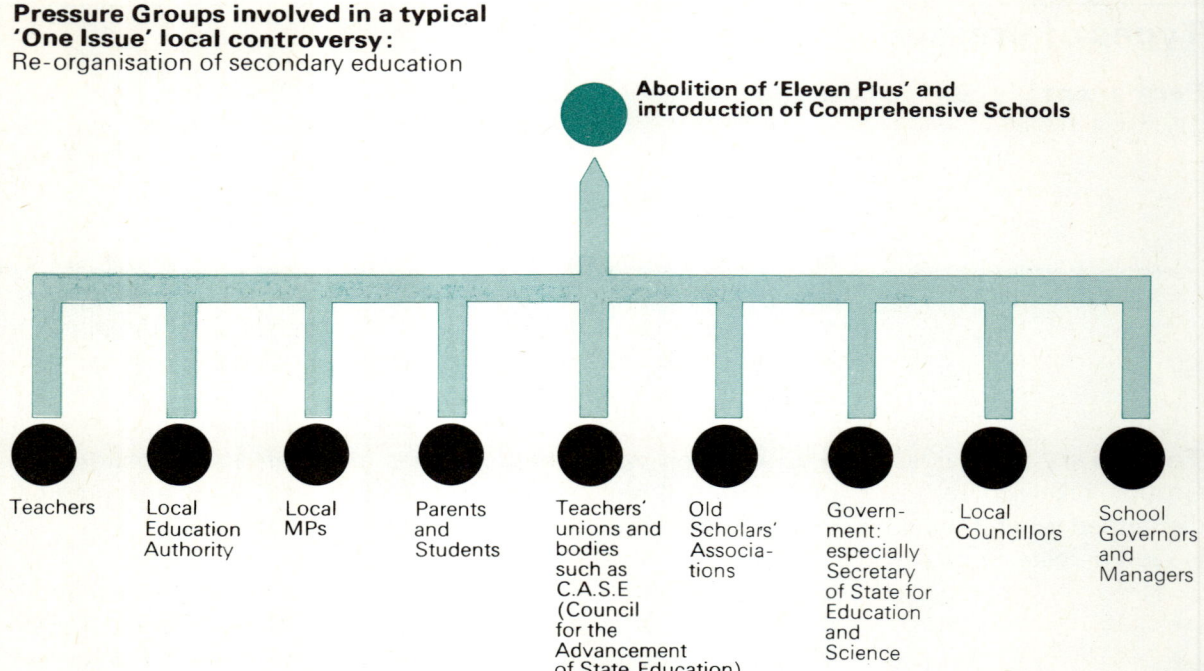

Abolition of 'Eleven Plus' and
introduction of Comprehensive Schools

Teachers | Local Education Authority | Local MPs | Parents and Students | Teachers' unions and bodies such as C.A.S.E (Council for the Advancement of State Education) | Old Scholars' Associations | Government: especially Secretary of State for Education and Science | Local Councillors | School Governors and Managers

Groups such as Teachers' unions and Old Scholars' Associations exist for other purposes; but some groups (including local teachers, parents and students) will become organised just over this issue.

newspapers were distributed, speakers toured the country to address mass demonstrations, and two of the League's main spokesmen became MPs and carried the campaign into Parliament. After seven years the League got its way, with the Repeal of the Corn Laws (1846), and promptly disbanded.

In the last 100 years or so the number of pressure groups has greatly increased. As society has become more complicated, the work of government has affected more aspects of life. And the more complicated society and government become, the more groups there are who have special interests to protect or causes to promote.

The diagram shows that pressure groups are formed over local as well as national issues. Parents, residents of an area, workers in a

factory, and many other such groups can be extremely effective. For instance mothers linking arms to stop traffic that endangers children, and then sending a petition to the council for a pedestrian crossing, stand a good chance of success. They may not think of themselves as being interested in 'politics'; but if they are trying to influence the policy of a local council they are directly involved in the political system.

How pressure groups work

Some pressure groups are represented, and listened to, at the highest levels of government. In fact each government department takes advice from what are called national advisory committees. One of these is the National Advisory Council for the Motor Manufacturing Industry. It includes representatives from the government, the trade unions and the employers, and its tasks are 'to provide a means of regular consultation between the government and motor manufacturers on such matters as

Newspaper circulation and politics, 1973 (Jan–June)

National dailies	Circulation per issue	Political persuasion
Daily Mirror	4 261 683	Labour
Daily Express	3 296 988	Conservative
Sun	2 931 466	Independent/Labour
Daily Mail	1 703 215	Conservative
Daily Telegraph	1 423 031	Conservative
The Times	345 044	Independent/Conservative
Guardian	344 356	Independent/reformist
Financial Times	194 651	Conservative
Morning Star	49 241	Communist

location of industry, exports, imports, research, design and the progress of the industry'.

Close contact with certain pressure groups is almost essential to modern governments, not just in making policies but in carrying them out. For instance if a decision had to be made about closing coal mines and making men redundant, the government would do its utmost to get the agreement of the National Union of Mineworkers. Failure to do so could lead to serious trouble, including protest strikes and a resulting loss of production. Some pressure groups give positive assistance to the government in carrying out its policies. For example the AA and the RAC help with the job of road signposting.

If possible, pressure groups like to have direct links with ministers and civil servants—who are at the centre of policy making. And ordinary MPs are useful allies too. Richard Crossman, a former Labour minister, described the situation as follows:

A considerable number of MPs on both sides of the Commons act as paid political agents of outside bodies . . . lobbying ministers on their behalf, and sometimes, when they rise to speak, reading aloud almost verbatim [word for word] the brief they have received from the body which retains their services.

Pressure groups that have close contact with ministers, civil servants and MPs gain special advantages. But it is difficult to say exactly how far these advantages go, because such groups often operate secretly. As a senior manager of a large company once put it, 'Whitehall is only two tube stations away: we have a permanent secretary to lunch from time to time.' Obviously groups which lack contacts of this kind, such as old age pensioners or housewives, find it much more difficult to get their views heard. There is a lot of talk about protecting their interests, but they would have more influence on government policy if they were better organised to fight their own battles.

Among the most powerful of all pressure groups are those which openly support one of the major political parties. The trade union movement for instance is the backbone of the Labour Party. Unions supply 80 per cent of Party funds and sponsor 40 per cent of Labour MPs. At the annual Labour Party Conference trade union representatives have by far the greatest voting power. On the other side, owners of private industry supply the bulk of Conservative Party finances. And many Conservative MPs are company directors.

Does this mean that governments can be dictated to by their supporting pressure groups? To some extent it does. But this is less sinister than it seems, because it is difficult to separate the interests of trade unionists and most Labour MPs, or businessmen and Conservatives. In both cases, pressure group and party share much the same principles.

Nevertheless when a party is in government it has a responsibility to the whole nation. No government likes to be accused of showing favouritism towards some groups at the expense of others. So in practice government policies do sometimes go against their own supporters. The Resale Price Maintenance Bill, introduced by a Conservative Government in 1963, abolished fixed prices for many goods sold in the shops and encouraged price cutting. It was strongly opposed by groups of shopkeepers and business-men (traditional Conservative supporters) yet it became law. No pressure group, however powerful or close to the government, can be *certain* of getting its way.

The mass media

In many countries the great majority of the people are poor and unable to read. Consequently newspapers have only a small circulation and expensive things like television sets are beyond the reach of most families (even if a television service is available). But the situation in Britain is very different. Practically every household takes a daily paper and has a radio and television set, so that the mass media are a vital element in political communication. What sort of influence do they have on politics?

The press

All newspapers have a definite 'point of view', which comes out not just in editorials but in the way they 'slant' the news. Most are politically biased towards one party. Some go further and publicise the opinions of just one man—the owner. For many years the political policy of the *Daily Express* and the views of its late owner, Lord Beaverbrook, were identical.

However there is little evidence to suggest that the press influences the way people vote. Most readers take a paper that is sympathetic towards the political opinions they already have. But it is likely that newspapers *reinforce* people's existing views, and encourage them to turn out and vote at election time. In this way the press could have an important influence on voting without actually 'converting' many people.

The press also plays a part in educating the public about politics—although some papers are much more informative than others. There is a world of difference between the detailed discussion found in the more 'serious' papers and the rather sketchy political coverage in the 'popular' press. But even where political reporting is very detailed, its true educational value is reduced if there is a strong bias towards the views of one party.*

The press is probably at its most effective in the protection of people's rights. It can be merciless in exposing scandal, corruption or just plain inefficiency by government departments, local councils and business companies. Indeed, many people who have a grievance look to the press as their first line of defence, rather than their MP.

Over the years there have been countless examples of successful newspaper 'campaigns'. One is described at the end of the chapter—the thalidomide case. Another which occurred shortly afterwards (1973) was a *Guardian* campaign about the pitifully low wages paid to black workers in British owned South African companies. It led to questions in Parliament, an investigation by a Commons committee and almost immediate increases in wages by one or two companies.

Even decisions at the heart of government can be affected by press comment. But the papers that have this sort of influence are not necessarily those with large circulations—they are the ones with the most influential *readers*. For instance *The Times* claims that it is read by 82 per cent of the civil servants and 76 per cent of the politicians listed in *Who's Who* (a guide to the

---

*The question of bias in news reporting is dealt with in *Enquiring About Society* (Series I)

nation's 'top people'). Other papers read by many important decision makers include the *Financial Times, Guardian, Telegraph, Sunday Times* and *Observer*; along with the political 'weeklies' such as the *New Statesman,* and the *Spectator.* Taken together, these papers provide an important 'platform' for political debate. Politicians *themselves* often contribute articles and readers' letters.

Broadcasting

The sorts of political 'campaigns' fought by the press are impossible in broadcasting because both the BBC and the commercial companies must remain neutral. In news reporting, equal weight is given to opposing arguments. And in any discussion of political issues it is usual for both major parties to be represented. However some documentary programmes do investigate social conditions critically, and pose awkward questions for the government. And of course the main parties are allocated time in which to present their *own* programmes, on both radio and television (see Chapter 3).

How much influence does broadcasting have on politics? Certainly the politicians themselves take it very seriously indeed, especially television. They realise that one false move in front of millions of viewers could be very damaging—

to themselves and to the public 'image' of their party. However skilful a politician may be in the Commons, he is always in danger of coming off second best in a confrontation with an experienced television interviewer.

Political broadcasting becomes especially prominent at election time. Party 'politicals' multiply, news bulletins give extensive reports on the progress of the campaign, and there are numerous election 'specials' on top of the regular current affairs programmes. All this, together with the marathon coverage of the results as they are declared, does much to inform the public about the workings of the political system.

But does television actually influence the way people vote? Unlike the press, the controllers of television channels do not themselves try to persuade people. However they do provide a political platform—interviewing party leaders, reporting their speeches and so forth. In this way television allows the *politicians* to influence

John F. Kennedy and Richard M. Nixon, the two candidates in the United States presidential election of 1960, meet face-to-face in front of TV cameras. This kind of confrontation in the mass media has always been avoided by party leaders in Britain.

the electorate—and that is what election campaigns are about. Television often brings together, face to face, politicians, experts in various fields, leaders of pressure groups and ordinary members of the public. This kind of 'mini-Parliament' can play a valuable part in political communication in modern society.

Two case studies of pressure group activity

Thalidomide

This was a medical drug developed in Germany and sold in Britain by a company called Distillers Ltd. In 1961 it was withdrawn from the market, when it was discovered that pregnant women who took it later gave birth to dreadfully deformed children. In all, about 400 such children were born in Britain.

Some of the parents involved took legal proceedings against Distillers, but this proved expensive and long drawn out. A public appeal was started for funds to help the children. Eventually, in 1968, Distillers offered about £1 million compensation to be divided among sixty-four of the children, provided all legal charges were withdrawn. They later said that they were willing to help the rest of the children too.

In 1971 the Company announced plans for a trust fund of £3·25 million. But they would give this money only if all the parents agreed. Five decided it was not enough. The Company then threatened to withdraw the offer unless the 'rebels' fell into line. However the five parents received support from the *Daily Mail*, which described Distillers' offer as 'Scandalous' in a front page article (December 1971).

Throughout 1972 the Company came under mounting pressure. The *Sunday Times* published a hard-hitting series of articles on the poor compensation terms. Jack Ashley, MP for Stoke-on-Trent South, took up the case in the Commons. And finally a group of Distillers shareholders formed a small pressure group inside the Company. Slowly Distillers raised their

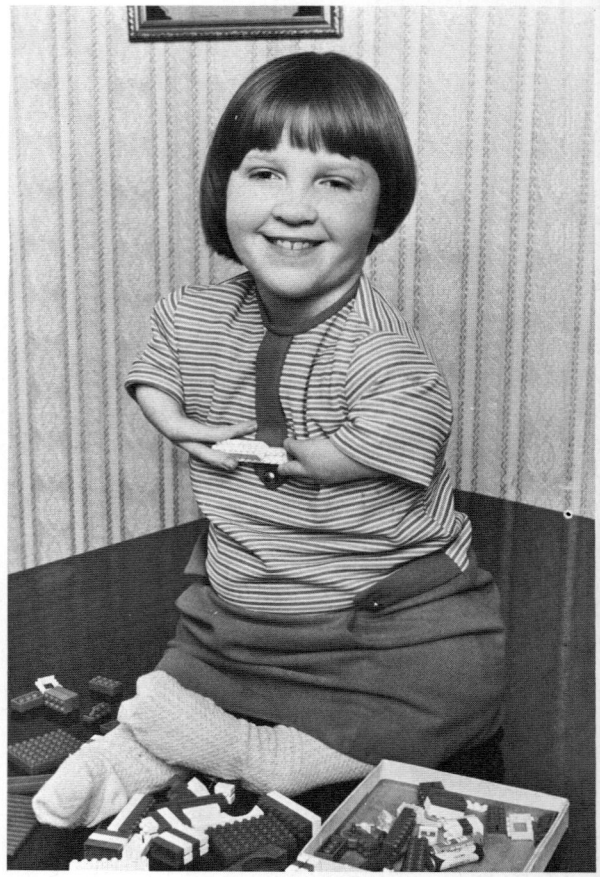

One of the 400 or so British victims of the drug thalidomide (which was withdrawn from the market in 1961). When taken by pregnant women, it led to the birth of babies with withered limbs and other deformities.

offer, until in the end they agreed to pay about £20 million over twenty years, through a trust fund.

Support from the press and others was a long time coming. But when it did come, things moved quickly. Almost certainly the compensation terms would not have reached £20 million without the efforts of the pressure groups. It should be added that successive governments refused to contribute any public money to help the thalidomide victims, although the National Health Service did give valuable assistance in fitting artificial limbs.

'Save the Avon Gorge'

In 1971 Bristol Corporation gave permission for a company to build a large hotel in the Avon Gorge, a steep-sided valley of outstanding natural beauty. The hotel was to be situated close to the famous and spectacular Clifton Suspension Bridge, built by Isambard K. Brunel in the nineteenth century.

The planning permission was discovered by a member of a local society concerned with preserving the character of the area. Without delay a meeting was called to discuss opposition to the scheme. It was attended by about twenty people, who called themselves STAG (Save the Avon Gorge). Local MPs were contacted, and questions asked in the Commons. The Minister for the Environment and the press were invited to investigate the matter, and posters and car stickers were distributed. Before long, letters of support were pouring in, and a petition was started. Various public figures were asked to help, and among others John Betjeman, the poet laureate, came to Bristol.

The Minister set up a public enquiry, con-

The Avon Gorge, spanned by Isambard Brunel's famous Clifton Suspension Bridge. The preservation of the natural beauty of the area was the subject of vigorous pressure group activity in 1971.

ducted by a planning inspector. It opened in May 1971 and lasted nine days. Opposing the hotel scheme were the National Trust and various local councils, together with individual architects and engineers. On the other side were Bristol Corporation officials, hotel representatives and some architects. In October the Minister accepted the findings of the Enquiry and permission to build the hotel was refused. STAG had won.

This case illustrates an important point about 'one issue' pressure groups. STAG won not so much because of the volume of public protest but because it managed to attract *influential* supporters. Most of its members were middle class, professional people, who knew *how* to organise themselves effectively and *where* to exert pressure.

To write, discuss and find out

1 'Nowadays it is hard to tell the difference between the two main parties.' Do you agree? Give reasons for your views.

2 Would you like to see a Coalition Government formed by the leaders of all parties in the Commons? What are

a the advantages;

b the disadvantages of this kind of government?

3 What sorts of arguments might pressure groups put forward on each of the following issues (both *for* and *against*)?

Arming the police

Removing the speed limit on motorways

Reintroduction of National Service

Raising the school leaving age to seventeen

Higher Old Age Pensions

Building a new ring road around a city

In each case, what do you think would be the most effective *methods* of exerting pressure?

4 Can you explain why the most effective pressure groups are not necessarily the noisiest?

5 Choose any well known politician and imagine that you are going to interview him (or her) on television. Make a list of questions you would ask

a if you wanted to show him in a good light;

b if you wanted to give him a rough time.

6 *Find out* the proportion of space devoted to politics in two contrasting newspapers—e.g. the *Times* and the *Sun*. Add up the total number of column inches in both papers, the column inches devoted just to politics, and then calculate percentage figures.

7 *Find out* how three or four newspapers, of contrasting political views, are reporting some controversial issue at the present time. Keep a scrapbook of cuttings which give evidence of political bias.

Much of this book has been concerned with Britain's political institutions — Parliament, prime minister and Cabinet, government departments and so on. However it was pointed out in Chapter 2 that to discover the true character of a political system it is necessary to examine the *underlying beliefs and principles* which back it up. And it was suggested that such principles could be brought to light by asking certain basic questions (turn back to Chapter 2 and look at them again). One question has been held back until now, however, because in many ways it sums up all the others. What is it that makes a system of government *democratic*?

The basis of democracy

Democracy is one of the most overworked words in politics. Nowadays just about every government in the world *claims* to be democratic, for one reason or another. This is hardly surprising, perhaps, since the word means 'the power of the people' (it comes from the Greek *demos,* which can be translated 'the people', and *kratos,* which means 'power'). So a government that calls itself 'democratic' is claiming that its right to rule is somehow based on the consent or agreement of the people.

There are few, if any, governments which would openly admit that they ruled without public consent. Even a dictator, with total power, likes to feel that his people support him—whether or not he gives them opportunities to show it. Indeed, many one-party states hold regular elections, although there is no real choice of candidates or policies. In 1962, elections in

North Korea actually produced a 100 per cent vote for the Workers' (Communist) Party.

How can we judge whether a system of government is truly democratic or not? Are there any 'tests' that can be applied? There is no general agreement on this, but we shall consider five principles which are particularly closely associated with democratic government. Together they provide some kind of measure or 'yardstick' of democracy.

Political freedom

In Chapter 1 it was argued that people cannot be given complete freedom to do anything they want. The 'freedom' to drive a car at 100 m.p.h. down the High Street is sacrificed in order to enlarge the freedom of the majority to cross roads fairly safely. However in a democratic state there are certain freedoms, closely linked to politics, which are limited as *little* as possible—freedom of speech, freedom to publish and freedom to meet and associate with others.

How far should limits on these freedoms go? Can we for example say exactly *how much* freedom of speech should be allowed in a democratic state? The answer must be no. In peacetime it is thought reasonable that people should be allowed to preach total non-violence. But this might not be allowed in the midst of a war, especially if it led soldiers to desert the army.

The important point is that the limits on various freedoms should be constantly debated. People's views do not always stay the same, and if a political system truly represents the 'power of the people' it must be able to reflect changing opinions. In the end, the most important aspect of political freedom is the right to openly discuss freedom itself.

Equality

People are obviously *un*equal in most respects —in height, weight, wealth, looks, intelligence and so forth. However equality does not depend on everyone being the same, or even being treated in the same way. The principle of equality simply means that where we treat people differently we should have *valid reasons* for doing so. And if we cannot give any valid reasons we should treat them equally. For instance it is generally accepted in a democratic society that there are no good reasons why some should have the right to vote and others be denied it—except in the case of children, criminals, the insane and so on, where valid reasons *can* be given.

The same argument applies to what is called 'equality before the law'. Two people who com-

American students protesting against their country's involvement in the Vietnam War in South-East Asia, 1969. Such demonstrations are only allowed in countries which have a large measure of political freedom.

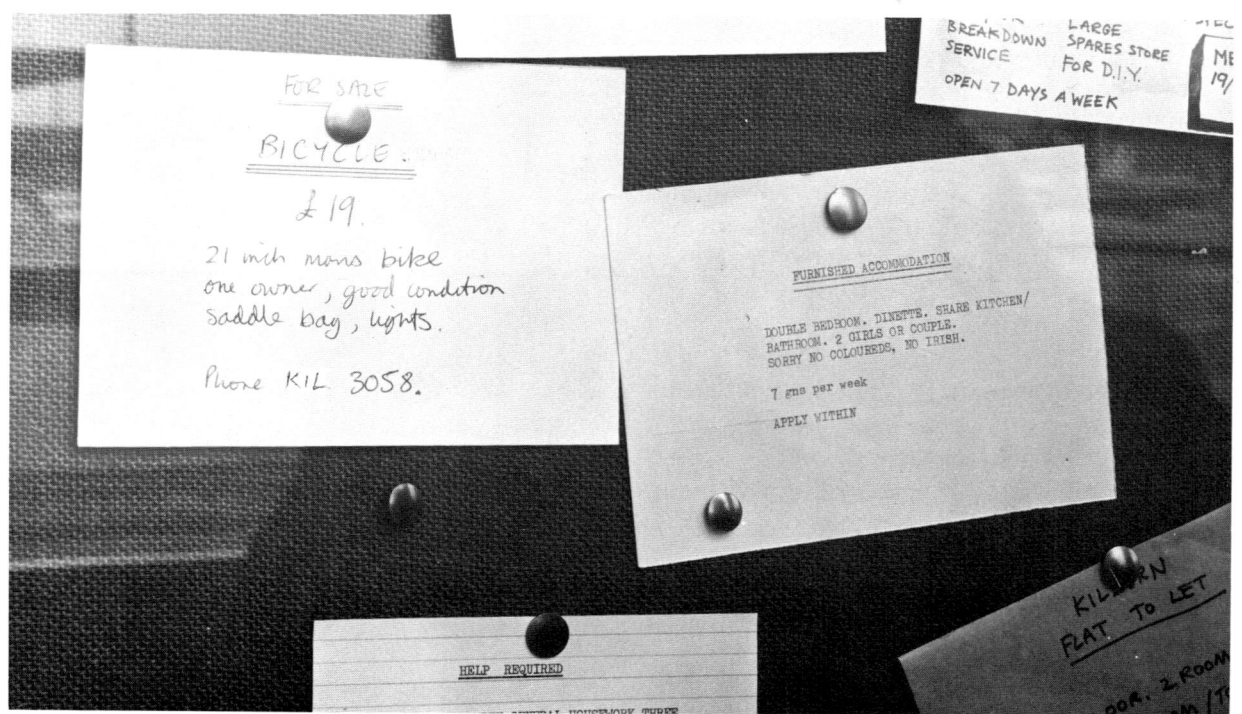

A notice of accommodation to let inserted in a shop window in the early 1960s. This kind of inequality through racial discrimination was later made illegal.

mit the same crime, in identical circumstances, should not be treated unequally because of differences in the colour of their eyes, the size of their bank balance, or any other 'reason' that is not relevant to the case. So arguments about equality boil down to arguments about how good the *grounds* are for treating people differently. To refuse a man a job because he is not qualified to do it is reasonable. But it is *un*reasonable to refuse him simply because he is red headed, a vegetarian, or black skinned. To do any of these things would be to go against the principle of equality.

Most arguments about equality are less straightforward. They involve not a simple choice between one thing and another but the problem of deciding how far equality should go. Differences in wealth are an example of this. In Britain there is still a wide gulf between the rich and ordinary people. And money can buy advantages—better medicine, a public school education, the best lawyers and perhaps a better chance of having political influence. How far should equality of wealth go in a demo-

cratic society? As with the limits on freedom, it is not possible to give a definite answer to this question. Again, what matters is that it is constantly debated, and that changes in the distribution of wealth are at least possible.

Openness

In what has been said about freedom and equality, the importance of public debate has been stressed. This in turn depends upon a certain 'openness'. Freedom of speech—in clubs and pubs, on television and in Parliament —is only a part of it. A democratic government should explain its thinking to the people, give reasons for its actions and try to gain public confidence. How else could it claim to have the consent of the people?

However most governments resort to secrecy in certain circumstances. In Britain, *D Notices* can be issued to prevent newspapers from publishing anything the government considers important to 'national security'. Some local councils try to exclude the public and the press from meetings. And secrecy can even extend to questions asked by MPs in the Commons. Ministers have been known to refuse to answer questions on such matters as the length of council house waiting lists, the collapse of a car insurance company, and arrangements for the purchase of drugs by the National Health Service. It is a task of MPs, pressure groups and the mass media to fight to keep secrecy to a minimum. In a democratic state people have a right to know what is going on in government.

Participation

If the people are to exert power on the government, it is necessary for them to *take part* in political affairs. The amount of participation in Britain varies from one situation to another. About four people in every five vote in general elections; but in local elections the turnout often falls to well under 30 per cent. According to social surveys, over four-fifths of the population claim to be 'not very interested in politics'. Certainly active membership of political parties is low (not above 10 per cent) and most pressure groups depend upon the efforts of a small core of organisers and spokesmen.

However before people can play an active part in democratic government they need a certain amount of political knowledge and experience. How is this gained? One way of getting valuable experience is to take part in such bodies as school students' councils, trade union branch meetings and local clubs and societies. Through these sorts of activities people learn how to state a case clearly, and appreciate the need to compromise and to accept majority decisions. Participation at this level is often a first stage in developing an understanding of local and national politics.

Of course people are much more likely to take an interest in political affairs if they feel that their views count for something. One way of

A school students' council: this is one way of gaining political experience.

directly involving the public in decision making is to hold *referendums,* in which each voter is asked to answer 'yes' or 'no' to a particular question. These are used in many countries to find out public opinion on an important issue. For instance in 1972 referendums were held in Denmark, Eire and Norway (but not in the United Kingdom) to find out if people wanted to join the EEC. The Norwegians said 'no' and Norway stayed out.

In some ways referendums are an attractive idea, because they allow the public to have the last word on an issue. Voting for a party in a general election is a less clearcut decision. Many voters find themselves supporting a particular party *in spite of* certain of its policies (some Labour voters for example are not in favour of nationalisation). General elections are held in Britain on average every four years. But important shifts in public opinion can take place in a much shorter space of time, and often totally new issues emerge during the life of a government. The only sure way of getting an up-to-date guide to public opinion, especially on a 'new' issue, is to hold a referendum.

Why, then, are referendums not favoured by British governments? In Britain it is believed that a government has a right or *mandate* to carry out its policies once it has won a general election. And MPs are expected not just to represent the views of constituents but also to use their own *judgment*. Besides, a government could use a referendum as a way of testing its overall popularity, by threatening to resign if the decision went against its policy. This would lead people to vote on party lines, as in a general election, and therefore blur the meaning of the referendum decision.

There are all sorts of ways of achieving public participation in politics. Referendums are just one of many possibilities.

Toleration

It was pointed out in Chapter 1 that a political system which allows disagreements to be openly expressed can only work if conflicting groups tolerate each other. To be tolerant of one's rivals does not involve liking or agreeing with them. It simply means that one accepts their right to be different—to hold opposing views and to express them publicly.

In a political system based on toleration, people are expected to settle their differences without hostility and violence. And the government is expected to use its powers to protect the

Referendums are rare in the United Kingdom. However in 1973 one was held in Northern Ireland, on the question of the border with Eire. Here we see Mr Brian Faulkner, Leader of the Ulster Unionist Party, watching the count in progress.

right of minority groups to be heard. This is an essential feature of all democratic governments, including our own. In fact the British like to think of themselves as one of the most tolerant of all nations. Our language is full of expressions illustrating this: 'live and let live', 'listen to the other fellow's point of view', 'give him a fair hearing', and so on.

If there is a spirit of give and take, democratic government is strengthened. But where fear or distrust of rival groups produces intolerance, then the necessary conditions for a democratic society quickly disappear. The recent history of Northern Ireland illustrates this. Hostility between Catholics and Protestants—with a Catholic minority long denied any real political influence—broke out into bitter street fighting in 1969. Within months, normal political life became impossible.

Politics and everyday life

The great majority of the British people are proud to say that they live in a democratic society. Yet at the same time most will admit that they have no desire to become 'involved' in

A disturbance in East London in the 1930s, involving Sir Oswald Mosley's Fascists—a group opposed to parliamentary democracy. This raises the question of how far toleration should go. Should it extend to those who aim to overthrow the political system?

politics—apart from voting in elections. This might seem to be a contradiction, but it is more likely a misunderstanding. People often do not realise that many of their day-to-day concerns, which they think of as 'non-political', are in fact very political indeed.

Governments have taken on ever-widening responsibilities in the last fifty years or so. And these affect the daily lives of everyone—in education, health services, employment, housing, industrial relations, the environment, roads, railways, prices, taxation, crime and so forth. There is no way of living in a society like ours and avoiding the consequences of political decisions.

When people's immediate interests in the family home or the workplace are threatened, they soon see the importance of politics in

their lives. People are not slow to protest about heavy lorries using side streets, houses being pulled down for roadbuilding, factories closing or cutting down their work force, and the like. They feel that they have a right to be heard, and expect to be treated fairly. In other words they come to see more clearly what it means to live in a democratic society.

How are political views formed?

Political opinions can be thought of in two ways. The most usual sense in which we talk of political views is in connection with party politics. Which side does a person support, and why? Underlying such views people also have opinions or beliefs about the *system* of government itself. In some countries large numbers of people have lost all faith in their political system. They believe that necessary changes can only come if the whole fabric of government is destroyed and a fresh start made.

There is no evidence to suggest that such views are widely held in Britain. Even during the 'Depression' of the 1930s, when the numbers of unemployed reached 3 million and poverty was widespread, there was little support for political revolution. The British have developed a peaceful and orderly style of

Unemployed men at a labour exchange during the 'Depression'. Even in those years there was little support for political revolution.

politics which has survived many crises and periods of stress.

Both kinds of political opinions—party preferences and attitudes towards 'the system'—are usually rooted in people's upbringing and social background. Right from early childhood we learn the ways of life of our society—moral rules, customs, values and so on—by mixing and communicating with other people. Sociologists call this *socialisation*.* We learn to live in society first from parents and other relatives, and then from teachers, friends, workmates and the mass media. And among the things we learn are basic political attitudes. We notice that people who disagree usually listen to each other's views and often try to reach a compromise. We find groups taking votes, accepting majority decisions and so forth.

This learning of political attitudes and behaviour expected in one's society is known as

---

*For a more detailed account of socialisation (and also a discussion of social class) see *The Family* (Series I).

Factors affecting voting behaviour

Main 'Socialising Influences'

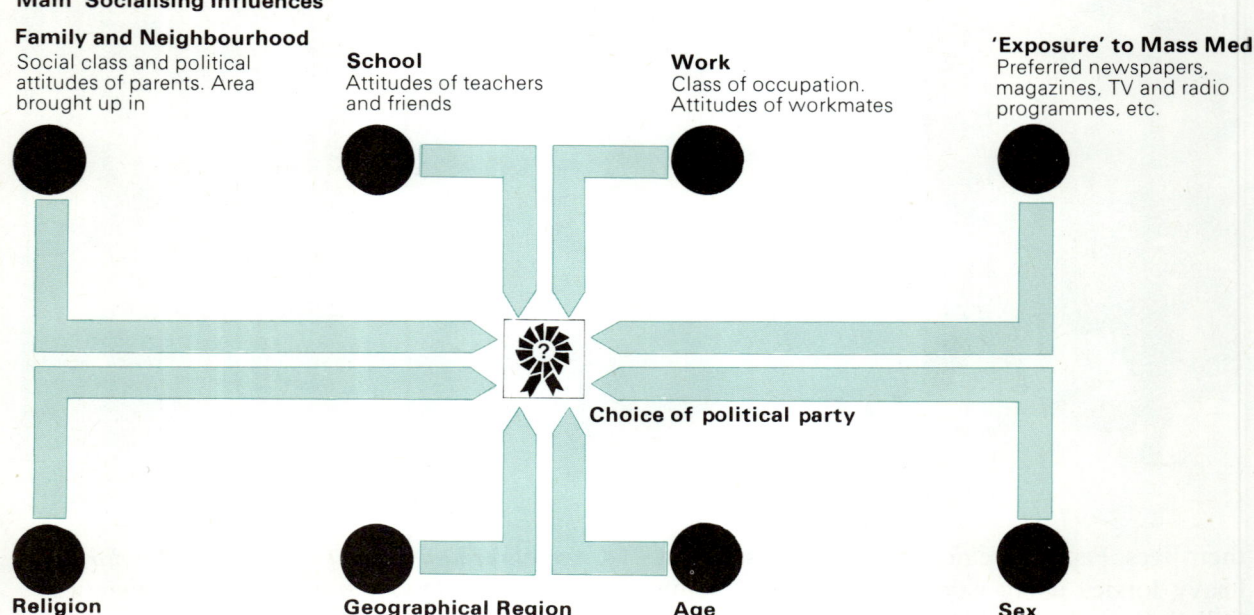

Family and Neighbourhood
Social class and political attitudes of parents. Area brought up in

School
Attitudes of teachers and friends

Work
Class of occupation. Attitudes of workmates

'Exposure' to Mass Media
Preferred newspapers, magazines, TV and radio programmes, etc.

Choice of political party

Religion

Geographical Region

Age

Sex

POLITICAL SOCIALISATION. In most cases it influences our views not just about the political system in general but also about parties and their leaders. We hear parents and friends talking about national politics and are inclined to accept the opinions of those we most respect. But not everyone is influenced in this way. People respond differently to similar socialising experiences. For example *most* people with Conservative parents vote Conservative too, but a number do not. The discussion of voting behaviour which follows is therefore based only on general trends among large groups of people. It does not (and, indeed, *cannot*) account for the views of every single individual.

Factors affecting voting behaviour

Socialisation and social class

The main socialising influences on an individual are shown in the top half of the diagram. All are politically important, but none more so than the family and neighbourhood. Attitudes

towards 'bosses', 'unions', and of course Labour, Conservative and Liberal, are often formed very early in life. And here the influence of parents is a vital factor. Research shows that the stronger the political views of parents the greater the influence they have on their children.

In a survey published in 1969 no less than 92 per cent of Labour voters interviewed came from families where both parents voted Labour. And 89 per cent of Conservative supporters came from families in which both parents were Conservatives. Where the party loyalties of parents were divided, their children's later voting patterns showed no strong trend towards one side or the other.* The political influence of parents is usually strongest at the time when their children first vote.

The influence of the family home is closely bound up with differences between *social classes* in voting behaviour. (Most people go on

---

*For further details, see David Butler and Donald Stokes, *Political Change in Britain* (1969).

Social class and political party

Whole population of United Kingdom   **Conservative voters**   **Labour voters**

Professional, business and 'white collar' workers: **The middle classes**

Skilled, semi-skilled and unskilled manual workers: **The working classes**

Proportions of the whole population

belonging to the same class as their parents when they grow up, so it is difficult to separate the two factors.) As the diagram shows, the majority of manual workers (those who work with their hands) vote Labour; and the majority of people in 'middle-class' or non-manual occupations vote Conservative.

Nearly two-thirds of the electorate are manual workers or wives of manual workers. So the Conservative Party needs to attract a lot of working-class support in order to win a majority of seats. How does this come about? Among a number of possible explanations of the 'working-class Conservative', two seem particularly likely. First, it seems that some working-class people look up to and respect the upper and upper-middle classes (most of whom are Conservatives) and believe that they are in some way 'born to rule'. Second, it appears that

quite a large group of manual workers— especially those 'coming up in the world'— *think of themselves as middle class* and vote the same way as most professional, business and 'white collar' workers.

Age

The table shows important differences in the voting behaviour of different age groups.

Voting in Britain, 1970 (National Opinion Poll) Percentage figures *(adjusted after election result)*						
Age group	18-24	25-34	35-44	45-54	55-64	65+
Conservative	42.3	41.0	46.1	43.3	47.5	56.2
Labour	47.2	45.8	40.6	49.1	43.7	37.1

How are these figures to be explained? It could be that people become more Conservative as they get older. But this would not explain the sharp increase in Labour support among the 45-54 age group. There is evidence that most people develop firm political views in the early years of adult life and then stick to them. If this is so, then a lot depends on the point in time when a person's voting habits are formed. Those over fifty-five in 1970 (the date of the survey) grew up at a time when the Labour Party was much less important than it is today.

Sex

Women are more likely than men to vote Conservative. Studies of Conservative voters in the four general elections from 1959 to 1970 show that the proportion of women was 12-14 per cent greater than the proportion of men. What effect does this have on election results? Research shows that on men's votes alone Labour would have won every election since World War Two.

Geographical region

Geography and voting behaviour are linked

Left *A typical area of strong Conservative support: the seaside town of Torquay, Devon.*
Above *A typical Labour 'stronghold': the industrial town of Merthyr Tydfil, Glamorgan.*

in two ways. First, in areas where there is a tradition of strong support for one particular party social class differences can be blurred. One study showed that in a mining area (a Labour stronghold) middle-class people were five times more likely to vote Labour than middle-class voters in a seaside town (a safe Conservative seat). Working-class people in the same seaside town were six times more likely to vote Conservative than working-class people in the mining constituency.

Secondly, there is an overall regional bias in voting. In Wales, Scotland and the North of England the majority of seats are Labour held (see the table in Ch. 2). The opposite is true of Southern England.

Religion

Only in Northern Ireland—where there is an overwhelming Protestant vote for the Unionist (Conservative) Party—does religion have a marked influence on voting. Nevertheless throughout the United Kingdom there is a tendency for members of the Church of England to favour the Conservatives. And the reverse is true of Nonconformist groups.

The reasons for some of these differences have never been explained satisfactorily. It is very

much easier to find out *what* happens in voting than to say *why* it happens. And to make the picture more complicated, voting patterns change in *by-elections* (these are held in seats which become vacant during the life of a Parliament). People who voted for the governing party in the previous general election often withdraw their support in a by-election if they are not satisfied with the government's record. The smaller parties frequently benefit from this, picking up large numbers of 'protest votes'. In recent years the Liberals and both Scottish and Welsh Nationalists have gained seats at by-elections. However most protest voters rediscover their former loyalties when the next general election comes round and the choice of a government is at stake.

To write, discuss and find out

1 *Democracy* is often defined as 'government *for* the people, *by* the people'. How far do you think this is a true description of the British political system?

2 Do you think *referendums* should be held in Britain? If you do, give some examples of recent political issues which could have been decided in this way. If, on the other hand, you are against referendums give reasons for your views.

3 Should there be any limits to toleration in a democratic society? For instance, what attitude should be taken towards revolutionary groups which preach the use of violence to overthrow the whole political system?

4 In Britain people can be prosecuted for discriminating against individuals on grounds of race or colour. What arguments can be used to defend such laws?

5 Can there be such a thing as democracy in a one-party state?

6 Do you think a school is, or could be, a democratic institution?

7 'The main threat to democracy in Britain is not that a dictator might seize power but that government could become too remote from ordinary people.'
Do you agree? Give reasons for your views.

8 Of all the *socialising influences* in your life, which do you think has had the greatest effect on your political opinions?

9 Refer back to the section on the Conservative and Labour Parties in Chapter 11, and then try to explain why a majority of working class people vote Labour and most middle class people support the Conservatives.

10 Write a profile of
a the typical Conservative voter;
b the typical Labour voter;
in terms of age, sex, class, religion and place of residence.

11 *Find out* when the next by-election is due, and when it comes collect press cuttings commenting on the outcome. Try to assess whether the result was in any way influenced by 'protest voters' deserting the major parties, especially on the government side.

Glossary of basic terms

Some of the most basic ideas or *concepts* (rules of thought) in politics have been printed in CAPITALS in the text. For easy reference they are listed here, with brief definitions.

COLLECTIVE CABINET RESPONSIBILITY Once a decision has been made by the Cabinet, all its members must accept responsibility for it and defend it publicly. Any individual not willing to do so should resign from the government.

CONSTITUTION A collection of rules and customs, usually written down, which control and limit the activities of governments (or other organised groups, such as clubs and societies).

CONVENTION An 'unwritten rule', custom or habit within a group or society. Many of the basic practices in British politics rest on conventions which have grown up over the years.

INSTITUTION A set of rules, standards and customs, known and expected within a particular society, which define certain ways of doing things.

MINISTERIAL RESPONSIBILITY A minister accepts responsibility for the actions of civil servants in his department. He is expected to answer complaints against officials made by the public through their MPs.

POLITICAL IMPARTIALITY Civil servants are expected to keep their private political views to themselves and work to the best of their ability for the government of the day. Similarly, the monarch does not 'take sides' in politics; she is expected always to act on the advice of the prime minister and government, whichever party is in power.

POLITICAL SOCIALISATION The learning of political attitudes and behaviour expected in one's society, and of opinions about party politics, through contact with parents and other relatives, teachers, friends, workmates and the mass media.

Further study

Books and other printed materials

The best sources of up-to-date political information, analysis and discussion are of course newspapers and periodicals. *Whitaker's Almanack* (published yearly) is an essential reference book, containing many pages of facts and figures about British politics, past and present. In addition, the following are recommended.

RUTH BRANDON, *Central Government*, Harrap, 1972 (New Generation series).

B. CRICK and S. JENKINSON, *Parliament and the People*, Hamish Hamilton, 1966 (Men and Movements series).

J. O. MURRAY, *State and People*, 5th edn, Harrap, 1967.

P. J. SIDEY, *Government and Politics*, Macmillan, 1966 (Nation Today series).

For more advanced readers
JACK HARVEY, *How Britain is Governed*, Macmillan, 1970.

J. W. HAWLEY, *Government*, Ward Lock, 1965 (Our Modern World series).

R. RHODES JAMES, *An Introduction to the House of Commons*, Collins, 1961.

D. M. PRENTICE, *Member of Parliament*, Ward Lock, 1963.

Historical background
R. J. COOTES and L. E. SNELLGROVE, *The Early Modern Age*, and *Britain Since 1700*, Longman Secondary Histories, 1972, 1968.

M. D. PALMER, *Government*, Batsford, 1970 (Past-into-Present series).

D. WARLOCK, *Parliament and the People, 1780–1970*, Nelson, 1970.

Packs of source extracts, with a linking commentary
STUDY GUIDES: (1) *Background to Britain: Political Institutions;* (2) *British Constitutional Monarchy;* (3) *Ask the Candidate.*
(Published by Study Centre Publications for Teaching Politics.)

Tapes

Parliament and the People, two $3\frac{3}{4}$ ips tapes, based on the book by B. Crick and S. Jenkinson (Students' Recordings).
The History of Government, three $3\frac{3}{4}$ ips tapes, based on the book by M. D. Palmer (Students' Recordings).
Our Democratic Heritage, series of tapes by the Central Office of Information: The Cabinet, How a Bill becomes Law, The Role of the Backbench MP, Political Parties in Britain. (Obtainable from The Resources Centre, Commonwealth Institute, Kensington High Street, London W8.)

16 mm films

Election in Britain (Distributed by Central Film Library, Government Building, Bromyard Avenue, Acton, London W3.) The electoral system and the role of political parties.
State Opening of Parliament (Central Film Library). Account of the Opening of Parliament, with historical background.
Member of Parliament (BBC TV Enterprises Film Hire, 25 The Burroughs, Hendon, London NW4.) The day-to-day work of an MP, in the Commons and in his constituency.

Filmstrips

The Story of Parliament (Visual Information Service.)
The Development of the Electoral System, Parts 1 and 2 (Common Ground).
Parliament Past and Present (*Daily Mail,* distributed by Educational Foundation for Visual Aids.)
Your Parliament (Educational Productions.)

Index

Page numbers in **bold** type denote illustrations